NINE LIVES AND COUNTING

NINE LIVES
AND COUNTING

A BOUNTY HUNTER'S JOURNEY TO
FAITH, HOPE, AND REDEMPTION

DUANE "DOG" CHAPMAN

#1 *NEW YORK TIMES* BESTSELLING AUTHOR

NELSON
BOOKS
An Imprint of Thomas Nelson

Nine Lives and Counting

Published in Nashville, Tennessee, by Nelson Books, an imprint of Thomas Nelson. Nelson Books and Thomas Nelson are registered trademarks of HarperCollins Christian Publishing, Inc.

Published in association with the Epic Agency, LLC.

Thomas Nelson titles may be purchased in bulk for educational, business, fundraising, or sales promotional use. For information, please email SpecialMarkets@ThomasNelson .com.

NOTE TO READER

THIS MEMOIR IS A TELLING OF THE LIFE OF DUANE LEE "DOG the Bounty Hunter" Chapman. It is a work of creative nonfiction. While all the stories in this book are true, dialogue has been re-created or added to ensure the narrative's flow and convey emotion. Some names and identifying details have been changed to protect the privacy of the people involved.

Much of Dog's life has been captured on film and television shows, in interviews, in articles, and in his two previous books. All these corroborate the timelines and main events presented here. This book tells some familiar stories but with a fresh perspective, and it ventures into the behind-the-scenes territory and backstories never shared with the public.

Between these pages, you will find priceless early memories of the author's childhood; never-shared glimpses at his life in prison, into his days as a single dad, and his job as a vacuum-cleaner salesman; and his story of learning to bounty hunt.

He tells the touching story of losing Beth to cancer and shares his grief candidly with readers. He gives an intimate look at meeting and marrying Francie Chapman—and this book holds another first-telling of a new twist for you as well. For all who are curious about what's been happening to and what's next for Dog the Bounty Hunter, this book will not disappoint!

CONTENTS

"Finally! Bone of my bone, flesh of my flesh!"
—Genesis 2:23 MSG

For Francie Patrice Chapman—
my woman sent from God

AUTHOR'S PREFACE

I HAVE MET MANY FAMOUS PEOPLE. I'LL NEVER FORGET WHEN I met William Shatner. We were headed to the same place and found ourselves walking up a flight of stairs together. He all but sprinted to the top, leaving me trailing behind.

"How old are you?" I asked when I caught up to him.

"Eighty-five," he answered.

"No way," I said. "There is no way you are eighty-five years old. You are in such good shape!"

At ninety-one, he wrote (another) autobiography because he had continued to learn and grow personally and wanted to leave a legacy that matters. He felt—even after an incredible acting career, being the author of nearly thirty bestsellers of fiction and non-fiction, and securing a permanent place in America's hearts as an icon—that he had not yet really done anything in his life worthy of being remembered. He had something more to contribute.

I understand his sentiment.

At seventy, I realize I will be gone someday, but this book

will still be here. These pages contain many of my memories and reflections. But more importantly, they follow my faith, which is now stronger and deeper than ever. As I wrote this book, I asked God if after I leave this earth and join the heavenly host, He will grant me the privilege of looking down to see anytime someone gives their life to Him after reading my story.

I was proud when I became well-known. I was prouder still when I became famous—and I even enjoyed being infamous. But now, what I want—what I care about—is leaving a legacy.

So for every biker, every convict, every addict and alcoholic, for every person who has been abused, every neglected child, and every broken, grieving, or hurting human, my prayer is that reading this book will touch your heart so much that you will be ready to call on God.

I promise He will answer.

And if I am already gone, and you are reading this, and you give your heart to Jesus, remember, I've asked Him to let me watch so I can celebrate your new life!

This book was written for you . . .

Dog the Bounty Hunter
March 2023

INTRODUCTION

A bend in the road is not the end of the road.

—Beth Chapman

I SAT IN THE STERILE HOSPITAL ROOM AS MY WIFE, BETH, beloved by millions of fans for her larger-than-life, feisty personality, lay emaciated. I crawled into her bed, cradling her in my arms, stroking her hair, and praying silently for a miracle. The room was plain—nothing like Beth's personality. Everything in it was some unimaginative shade of white or tan. It had that sanitary, antiseptic smell and was lit by those harsh fluorescent bulbs that make even healthy people look sick.

My vibrant Bethy was trapped in her bed, hooked up to monitors and IVs to help manage the pain of the cancer ravaging its way through her body. She had originally been diagnosed with stage 2 cancer of the throat—a squamous cell carcinoma, they called it. From the moment she received this diagnosis, I simply would not tolerate anything negative being spoken about it.

"Duane, I know you love to be positive about everything," Beth said. "But sometimes it annoys me—like you are living in a fairy tale or something—but facts are still facts. I have cancer."

I have always held that the tongue is the most unruly member of the body, and I was taught that death and life are in the power of the tongue.[1] I refuse to speak about death or let anything negative come out of my mouth. As a child, if I told my mother I had a bad cold, she would respond, "Duane, you don't have a bad cold— you have the *symptoms* of a bad cold."

If I told her my tooth hurt so bad it was falling apart, my mom would say, "Claim that, and it's yours. Instead, say you have a tooth that needs attention."

I still hold to this conviction, so when Beth would state, "I have cancer," I would reply, "Bethy, don't say that. You do not have cancer; you have the *symptoms* of cancer, do you hear me?" I didn't want her to claim that cancer was hers. I wanted her mind to fight it, not agree with it.

Words are just your thoughts expressed, and they are powerful.

I was sent home in first grade because I couldn't stop crying when I heard the Humpty Dumpty nursery rhyme. My mom told my teachers the next day that I couldn't handle the fact that Humpty's egg had cracked everywhere and couldn't be put back together again. My teachers let me rewrite the rhyme and teach it to the class. I stood in front of all the first graders and recited my version of the poem:

> Humpty Dumpty sat on a wall,
> Humpty Dumpty had a great fall.
> All the king's horses and all the king's men
> Got together to put Humpty together again.

When the class heard the new ending, they all clapped and cheered. From then on, that was the way the poem was taught in my school.

I also made my mom change that prayer, "Now I lay me down to sleep, I pray the Lord my soul to keep, if I should die before I wake, I pray the Lord my soul to take." It didn't give me the comfort intended to help a child sleep peacefully. "If I should die before I wake" was fuel for bad dreams, so I made Mom take out the bit about death. My dad mocked me for it, but my grandpa told me, "Duane, that's just your personality."

I have carried that philosophy with me throughout my entire life. I even had ministers change my marriage vows to take out the "till death do us part" phrase because I didn't want to speak death in any way, shape, or form over my life or over my marriage. I have never allowed anyone close to me to speak negative words over or curse themselves in my presence. So anytime Beth would say words that owned cancer or say anything to me about dying, I would reject it.

After her diagnosis, our lives changed. We filmed an emotional two-hour special for A&E called *Dog and Beth: Fight of Their Lives*, which was grueling. It's still hard to watch. The crew captured intensely personal moments of us trying to deal with the uncertainty and all the decisions we had to make. In an emotional phone call when we broke the news to our kids and grandkids, I sent Beth away as I told the family, "We are gonna show the world how she's gonna beat this, okay?"[2]

It was an incredibly stressful time as we struggled to cope with the news, and there were so many details to take care of that it was overwhelming. The famous television series *Dog the Bounty Hunter* and *Dog and Beth: On the Hunt* had both ended. Our medical insurance was through the Screen Actors Guild, which required a certain number of hours spent performing to maintain eligibility.

On the day after Beth's surgery, I had to fly to Honolulu to fulfill a contract to appear as a guest on *Hawaii Five-O*. Leaving her was so hard, and her anxiety at my leaving was multiplied by her pain and the effects of the anesthesia and medication, so sometimes she said things that were very unlike her. But I was so excited about seeing her when I returned to LA that I didn't care what she said or called me.

So much of our life—our highs and our lows—had been lived out on air as it happened. This was no different. In that A&E special, I took the call live to learn the pathology results after her surgery. "Hello, attention!" I cleared my throat as I walked into the kitchen to deliver the news.

"No cancer!" I exclaimed, and everyone broke into relieved cries of joy and applause.[3]

Facing something this threatening makes your priorities clear. Beth had been given a second chance, and I wanted to make the most of it and make the next years with her the best years with her.

———

After the doctors reported getting all the cancer out, I was certain we had our miracle. The worst was surely behind us. The doctors had told her to take it easy, but Beth being Beth—strong-willed and determined—she hadn't listened. Initially after surgery, Beth wanted to give up bounty hunting and bail bonding altogether. But we had been on television for fifteen years. Without a mic on, I was unemployed! I kept on bounty hunting, though, and sometimes we would make the most magnificent arrests, and I would say, "Damn! Where's the camera?"

Just a year after Beth's surgery, the cancer returned, but this time it was diagnosed as stage 4 and had spread to her lungs. Her doctors urged her and her friends insisted that she undergo chemotherapy, but after just one treatment, she became violently ill. Her doctor had told her plainly, "You have an incurable disease," and she could see so little possible benefit and so many terrible side effects to this treatment that she decided to stop the chemo. She wanted to be Beth right until the end—feisty and fighting.

I was still holding out for a miracle.

She came up with an idea for a new television series. She felt she was a big part of why our last show had been canceled—some irreconcilable differences with the network. I remember her saying, "Big Daddy, you are famous, but you could be a legend!" She was a big motivator behind us putting together *Dog's Most Wanted*, which was picked up by WGN. And it was personal. I was fighting that disease with every violent criminal we chased across the country. I was fighting for Beth and chasing hope.

With no other way to get rid of or stop the spread of the cancer, her pain became so severe that the only way she could manage it was by using CBD oil and drinking alcohol. She often asked me to fix her martinis to numb the pain and help her forget about the cancer for a little while. It tore me up to see her like this, and I barely left her side for those last two years.

She never stopped fighting, though. Even in the final weeks of her life, she fought with the doctors to let her fly to a health spa for three weeks with her good friend Shannon Tweed, Gene Simmons's wife. The doctors refused to let her get on an airplane, telling her she wouldn't survive the trip. They told her she wouldn't be alive in sixteen days. Beth defiantly went to get a steroid shot and packed for the trip anyway. As she was packing, she stopped breathing and fell to the floor. I called 911 and began giving her mouth-to-mouth until the paramedics came.

When the ambulance arrived and took her to the hospital, they said she had a complete block in her throat. It took five doctors to successfully intubate her so she could breathe again. They kept her sedated—a medically induced coma—because the pain was so bad. Whenever they would try to let her wake, she would attempt to claw the tube from her throat.

In one of her last moments of lucidity before this, I had heard her raspy voice calling to me. "Big Daddy," she said weakly, her big brown eyes looking at me.

"Yes, Beth?"

"God's taking me out of your life."

"What?" I asked, still unwilling to entertain the idea that she was dying despite what the doctors had said. "Don't talk like that. God's gonna—"

"No, listen to me!" she interrupted with an intensity that comes only when someone knows their time is almost up. "You know you're called to be a minister. I'm stopping you. I'm standing in your way—"

"Beth," I agonized.

Her eyes held mine. "Listen, God is taking me out of your life for a reason, Big Daddy. *Don't* let me down. Don't you *dare* let me down. You got that?"

"Yes, Beth," I promised, tears streaming from my eyes.

Her final days in intensive care are still a blur. On Wednesday, June 26, 2019, I tweeted, It's 5:32 in Hawaii, this is the time she would wake up to go hike Koko Head mountain. Only today, she hiked the stairway to heaven. We all love you, Beth. See you on the other side.

It was hard to accept that she was gone. I recalled the words of Jesus when they told Him about Jairus's daughter. "Stop wailing,"

Jesus said. "She is not dead but asleep."[4] So that is how I choose to view Beth. I will see her again in heaven. She is not dead. *E moe ana*—she's sleeping.

———

My mother was a Sunday school teacher with the Assemblies of God, and from the time I was six years old, people had spoken over me that I would preach the gospel. I became famous for my "backseat" ministry to fugitives on *Dog the Bounty Hunter.* Throughout my marriage to Beth and all the shows we did together, I made concessions regarding my faith, sometimes compromising it in pursuing fame. I have been a one-foot-in and one-foot-out Christian for most of my life.

From the days when I was part of the Devil's Diciples (that's spelled d-i-c-i-p-l-e-s, not like the biblical disciples) motorcycle gang robbing and stealing, to the time I was in a Texas prison as an accessory to first-degree murder and started praying for the other inmates, to my six marriages, I became an expert at making excuses for a lot of the things I did. I got really good at asking God for forgiveness. Don't get me wrong; I've always loved God and had a really strong faith, and I never stopped hearing God talk to me. I just chose to be a Christian when it was convenient for me.

That all changed after Beth's death.

After Beth's passing, I was a lost and angry man. I was angry at the doctors for not being able to save her. I was angry at the whole medical system for letting us down.

We did a funeral for her in Hawaii and later a bigger memorial service in Colorado; then everybody went back home. I was alone.

For the first time in decades, I was completely by myself. I had no idea where anything was. I was lost inside my own kitchen; I couldn't find anything, let alone think of what I was supposed to be doing about the business. I couldn't think straight. I became so low and so depressed I was desperate. My world was rocked, and I was shaken to my core.

One night I had a dream. I saw Beth watering the grass in heaven. I walked up to her, and she turned around and said, "Big Daddy, what took you so long?"

She's waitin' for me, I thought. *I'm supposed to be up there with her.* I even thought, *How can God handle her without me there to help Him!?*

When I woke up, my mind flashed back to the hundred or so guys I'd chased down for violating restraining orders against them. Time and again, they would look at me, sometimes crying, and say things like, "I love her. I gotta see her, don't you understand?"

Well, now I did. I felt the same way. *If Beth had a restraining order on me,* I thought, *there would be no cop, no threat of jail or consequence that would keep me from seeing her.*

My next thoughts grew dark. *What's the best way to kill myself so I can join her?* I pondered.

And I almost did.

Later that night, I considered ending it all. As I contemplated how to do this, I heard the Lord say, *Don't you dare, Dog. Don't you take the life I've given you!*

Lost and angry, I threw a glass across the room. *Maybe I should go back to my biker-gang life.* All the good I had done to help bring criminals to justice didn't seem to matter. Nothing seemed to matter. I was numb on the inside. Days and nights ran together, and I felt I had lost my purpose. Maybe if I went back to the gang, I would just die in a blaze of . . . not glory, but die in a blaze of *something* and get to see Beth . . .

Several weeks after Beth's funeral, I started really studying the Bible—not just reading a verse here and there for comfort. I was hungry to read God's Word. Slowly, I began to emerge from my dark place. I reached out to some people for help because all that isolation was torment. I found myself some good, strong Christian mentors to hold me accountable. I had told Beth I would never marry again, but she knew I would. She told me that it was not good for me to be alone.

She was right.

Since I was first married at nineteen, I have always had a woman to share my life with. I met Francie, who had also lost her spouse, and we began bonding as friends over our grief. I married her about two years after Beth passed. I knew exactly what I wanted in a mate. I wanted a Jesus-loving, bold Christian woman who would help me on my newly rededicated path of faith. God brought me my Francie, and she has been an answer to every prayer I prayed.

I think Beth would approve.

———

As I turn seventy, I have a new lease on life. I have renewed purpose. I feel like King Hezekiah when the prophet Isaiah told him to put his house in order because he was going to die.

See, Hezekiah had an illness—a serious illness—and the prophet gave him the bad news that he wasn't going to recover. Instead of accepting that, Scripture records that Hezekiah turned his face to the wall, wept bitterly, and prayed to the Lord. Before

Isaiah had even made it all the way out of the temple, God sent him back to tell Hezekiah his prayers were heard, and he had been granted another fifteen years to live—borrowed time.

This might sound harsh, but I believe Hezekiah wasted his borrowed time. You can read about it in 2 Kings 20 and 2 Chronicles 32. Long story short, Hezekiah was content to spend his extra fifteen years building up his own riches and enjoying the perks of being king. When Babylonian emissaries visited, Hezekiah showed off all his wealth—making Judah a very tempting target for Babylon, which was on the rise at that time.

Through the prophet Isaiah, the Lord rebuked Hezekiah for being a prideful showoff and told him in no uncertain terms, "The time will surely come when everything in your palace, and all that your predecessors have stored up until this day, will be carried off to Babylon. Nothing will be left. . . . And some of your descendants, your own flesh and blood who will be born to you, will be taken away, and they will become eunuchs in the palace of the king of Babylon."[5]

Hezekiah's response? "'The word of the LORD you have spoken is good,' Hezekiah replied. For he thought, 'Will there not be peace and security in my lifetime?'"[6] In other words, Hezekiah didn't care much about his descendants or his legacy. He was content to enjoy his fifteen years of borrowed time and God's guarantee of peace and safety within the span of his own years.

I do not intend to waste my extra years of borrowed time. Where Hezekiah was content to concern himself only with what would happen to him in his lifetime, I have a burning desire to pass the blessings of God's love and power to the next generation. I want to see souls brought into the kingdom. I want to make sure my testimony glorifies God and that everything I do from this day forward is wrapped in His purpose and His plans for me.

There is nothing I enjoy more than seeing someone commit their life to Christ. If I am in a meeting and I see someone stand up to answer an altar call, I can't help it—I jump up on my feet and walk down that aisle with them. Seeing a life changed is the biggest high ever! I want to make the most of the time I have left for the kingdom. I have not been the best Christian throughout my life—and most of that has been documented on camera for the world to witness—but now everything is different. I am not the same man I was; I have been reborn.

You may think you know Dog the Bounty Hunter. Think again. This time, I'm writing my story—my way.

I will always hunt down fugitives to make them accountable to the law. Now I am also hunting down the outcast, the leper, the lame, and the brokenhearted. I am hunting the prisoner, the trafficked, the addict, the dysfunctional. I want to see them reborn too. This is the Dog I was called to be.

"Go into all the world and preach the gospel to all creation."[7]

ONE

PUPPY
PAINS

Train up a child in the way he should go,
And when he is old he will not depart from it.
—Proverbs 22:6

LONG BEFORE I BECAME AN OUTLAW, I WAS A GOOD CHRISTIAN kid. I grew up in church and accepted Jesus Christ into my heart when I was around five or six years old. My mom was a devout Assemblies of God Sunday school teacher and minister who brought me to church with her every Sunday. Now, maybe you grew up in a Baptist, Lutheran, or Catholic church, or maybe your family didn't attend any church at all. But my roots are in the Pentecostal church—where people expect to experience God's presence tangibly. They worship by singing, shouting, dancing, clapping their hands, and yes, even praying in tongues.

None of this was strange to me; it was as normal as learning my ABCs. The people there were open to hearing from God in ways that guided their everyday lives. Many verses in the Bible talk about prophecy, and our church practiced "you can all prophesy one by one" literally.[1]

Some women in the church prophesied over me that I would be called to ministry and have millions of followers. This was *way* before the internet and long before social media. I didn't even know how many zeros you needed to write one million as a number, let alone comprehend what a million people represented. Our congregation had only about three hundred members, which seemed like a *huge* crowd to me as a child.

And ministry? You mean like a fire-and-brimstone preacher? No thanks. That didn't really appeal to my tracking, fishing, football-loving, wild-at-heart boyhood. Yet here I am, more than sixty years later, with millions of followers across my platforms, and I freely share about Jesus on all of them. I guess those church ladies heard right!

Every week, our pastor would ask if anyone in the congregation had a testimony to share before the sermon. When I was eleven, my mom encouraged me to stand up. One of the first testimonies I remember sharing was when I needed sixty dollars to buy clothes for school. At the time, Grandpa Mike had the biggest delivery service for the *Rocky Mountain News* in Colorado. Every morning, he would take me with him on his route, and we would throw the papers. We started at 4:00 a.m. and would throw hundreds of papers every single day. At the end of the month, we would drive around to collect the three-dollar subscription fee from each house we delivered to.

While we were out collecting, I prayed and asked God to provide the sixty dollars I needed. I didn't know how He would do it, but I had faith that if I asked Him, He would find a way. I walked up the sidewalk of a modest little home and knocked on the screen door. The lady of the house answered the door with a big smile on her face. "Hello there, Duane Lee," she said.

"Good afternoon, ma'am," I answered politely.

"I don't know why, young man, but the Lord told me to give you a check for sixty dollars. Can you stay right there for a minute?" she asked.

I nodded.

She stepped into her living room and returned shortly with a stack of bills folded in her hand. "I happen to have it in cash. Is that okay?" she asked, handing me six ten-dollar bills. That was the biggest stack of money I'd seen in my life!

So when the pastor asked for testimonies that following

Wednesday, I stood up. I relayed my story to the congregation. When I finished, the pastor asked, "Where in the Bible does it say that God will provide for your needs?"

My mind raced to think of scriptures I had memorized in Sunday school, but I wasn't quite sure of the chapter and verse, so I looked over at my mom for help. From her pew, I could see her mouthing at me, "Exodus 11."

"In Exodus," I offered.

"There is a good one in Exodus, son!" the preacher clapped me on the back. "In Exodus 11:2, it says, 'Speak now in the ears of the people, and let every man borrow of his neighbor and every woman of her neighbor, jewels of silver and jewels of gold.' That certainly sounds like an ample supply for any need."

I nodded my head yes.

To me, the cash my neighbor had given me was as good as gold, and it was an *exact* answer to my prayer. The congregation applauded and whooped and hollered, "Praise God!" Their approval felt good. Being in front of an audience felt good, and from then on, I would share a testimony with the church at least twice a month.

Most people are terrified of public speaking, but I never was. I loved it. I was the only kid they regularly asked to give a testimony. I thought it was because my mom was a secretary and accountant at the church, and she played the organ—I assumed it came with the territory. It wasn't until much later that I realized it was a special privilege I'd been given.

———

I loved spending time with Grandpa Mike. One time we were watching the TV show *Fury*, a Western about a horse named Fury.

It was my favorite show: "the story of a horse and the boy who loves him." I thought having a horse was probably about the coolest thing on the planet. I really wanted a horse—just like Joey Clark had on the show.

My mom and grandpa often quoted, "If ye shall ask any thing in my name, I will do it,"[2] and when I had asked God for sixty dollars, He came through. That had built my faith. If God could give me sixty dollars for clothes, why not a horse? So I prayed and asked God for a horse named Fury. I didn't tell anybody about my prayer. It was just between God and me. About three weeks later, Grandpa Mike bought a Shetland pony and surprised me with it.

"What are you gonna name it?" he asked, patting down the pony's haunches.

"Fury!" I shouted. My excitement could not be contained. I had a horse of my very own!

My mom often took me with her to minister on the Navajo Nation Reservation. Spending so much time on the reservation, I had grown to love horses and riding. I rode that little Shetland pony till I got too big for him to carry me. I couldn't wait to share this testimony with the church, and when I did, the pastor asked, "Duane Lee, now, in the Bible, does it say you can have a horse?"

This time I was prepared. I rubbed my chin thoughtfully for effect, then answered, "Well, not exactly. But in John 15:7, it says, 'If ye abide in me, and my words abide in you, ye shall ask what ye will, and it shall be done unto you.'"

The pastor smiled and nodded his head in affirmation. My mother was beaming.

While it was true that I liked the attention of getting up in front of the congregation to tell my testimonies, it was also true that having my specific prayers answered like this confirmed my belief that God was real and that He cared about me. I have never questioned this.

———————

Colorado, Utah, Arizona, and New Mexico all have Indian reservations and many indigenous people. We went to a chapel on the Navajo Nation reservation whose congregation was made up of Apache. There are many Apache Christians, and there is even a Bible translated into the Apache language.[3] Services at this chapel were pretty much the same as the ones held in the white church— singing, dancing, clapping hands, praying in tongues, preaching (though way less fire and brimstone), and prophecy. My mom took me there frequently.

I often sang special numbers while she played the piano, then Sister Jensen, my mom, or Aunt Iris would speak. One afternoon during an altar call, one of the elders approached Mom and me and said, "This half-breed here, he will preach and influence millions of people. Millions will follow him." Then he laid hands on me and spoke a blessing.

My mother taught me that anyone who bled red was my brother. She loved that I made friends with two young men, Titus and Mescal, and Titus and I became best brothers. Everyone on the reservation called me "Breed," even though my mother was a "Round Eye" (white). I used to ask her why they called me that, and she would just say, "That's good, son. Don't you worry about it. It means you are the best of both worlds. It's the French Indian in you."

Now, to me, my mother was the purest saint who ever walked

the earth. It never entered my mind that she could or would tell me a lie. I had no idea that she wasn't French Indian—that she wasn't any kind of Indian at all. But she always told me she was French Indian, which made me part Indian too.

"Am I Apache?" I asked, but she just hugged me tightly. I never questioned her about it again because I felt at home on the reservation. The Apache treated me like I belonged, and it felt good to be one of them, even if they did call me Breed (which really meant half-breed).

Deepening my core belief that I was Indian, through the sixth grade, I lived in an area where they bused white children to a Mexican school. I stood in line with all the Latinos for lunch and was handed a yellow card. I thought the card meant I was half Mexican. I was confused, so I asked one of my teachers if I was Mexican.

"No, Duane, you are not Mexican; you are Indian," she said, which made more sense to me since they called me Breed on the reservation.

Whenever the neighborhood kids played Cowboys and Indians (which you could still do in the 1960s), I always wanted to be one of the Indians. My time playing on the reservation was a far different experience from the strict rules and the fire-and-brimstone teachings I heard weekly at our church. When other kids got pop guns and holsters for Christmas, Grandpa Mike gave me a bow and arrow or a tomahawk. My dad was white, but my mom told me so often that she was French Indian, and I never questioned that I was part Indian.

It wasn't until much later (in 2016), when my sister Jolene was near death, that she told me my dad, Wesley Duane Chapman, wasn't my real father. I have since taken a DNA test to determine my origins, and it came back 33.33 percent Chiricahua Apache. I learned my biological father was Apache.

As I got a little older, I got bored of hearing the same message about going to heaven or hell over and over again. One Sunday, I complained about the repetitiveness of the sermons, and my mom told me, "Son, it's not going to be for you every time. You may get a sentence out of it, but when one man gets saved by the message, the angels in heaven throw a party."

I loved the idea of the angels throwing a party when someone got saved, but I was still bored hearing the same salvation sermon every week.

Sometimes, after service, the pastor and some of the church elders would take someone who was demon possessed into the prayer room and cast the demons out. Deliverance was a lot less boring to me than sermons. My curiosity was high as I listened outside the door and heard the person start howling. It made the hair stand up on the back of my neck.

I found it amazing that the person would come out a little later, "clothed and in their right mind."[4] They were totally normal. My mom was routinely asked to pray during one of these sessions, and I used to beg her to let me come with her. I could tell when a person was demon possessed. I could see it in their eyes. Finally, when I was twelve, my mom let me start going with her into the prayer room.

Inside, as many as twenty people might surround the possessed person. It wasn't always dramatic, but sometimes the person would start to growl, and their face would contort as they writhed around while we rebuked the demons. Occasionally while I prayed, God would share things with me. Sometimes I knew that the person who came in for deliverance was an alcoholic or that he beat his wife. My mom would often already know these things, but she was amazed that God had given me the spiritual gift of knowledge—spiritual insight into situations.[5]

As we prayed, the presence of God was powerful. It seemed to me it might have been like being in the fiery furnace with Shadrach, Meshach, and Abednego when King Nebuchadnezzar looked inside. He expected to find these three sons of Israel all dead, burned up. Instead, he was astonished and cried out, "Look! . . . I see four men loose, walking in the midst of the fire; and they are not hurt, and the form of the fourth is like the Son of God."[6] It felt so real.

The longer and more intensely we prayed together in the prayer room, the more it really did seem like Jesus was in there with us, and the room seemed to get brighter. Then the person we were praying for would stop growling, writhing, and contorting, and this smile would cross their face. They would get perfectly still as peace filled them. I could see a visible difference in their countenance; the person was always very grateful. It never really scared me to engage in that kind of spiritual warfare, because I saw how God was bigger than every demon we prayed against.

I knew that if God was with me, whatever was against me was going down!

Of course, not everyone believes there are still demons on the earth tormenting people in the twenty-first century. A lot of Christians don't even believe that deliverance, as practiced in the Bible, is still necessary today. But it seems funny to me that Christians seem more skeptical about the demonic and demon possession than the world. It is also interesting that I meet people who don't believe in God but do believe in demons.

I have worked in show business for decades. People's fascination with darkness is big business in Hollywood. I promise, in my real-world encounters with criminals and addicts as a bounty hunter, I have seen what oppression by demons does to people. It is real. Satan is the enemy of your soul, and just as God has angels who bring us His messages and protect us, the devil has demons who bring us damaging messages to torment and harass us.

Evil is real.

But the good news is that God is also real, and He has infinitely more power than Satan. We don't know for sure, but the book of Revelation implies that only one-third of all the angels ended up following Satan and becoming what we call demons, with the remaining two-thirds staying true to God—you can read about that in Revelation 12, especially verses 4 and 9. If that's the case, there are two angels for every one demon. The devil is outmatched and outclassed—any way you look at it!

My mother was diligent in teaching me Bible stories, but more than that, she had a way of breaking down some of the core doctrines of our faith so that I could understand them, even as a child. She taught me about the nine manifestation gifts of the Holy Spirit: the word of wisdom, the word of knowledge, the gift of faith, and the gifts of healings, miracles, prophecy, discerning of spirits, different kinds of tongues, and interpretation of tongues.[7]

I wanted to accept the Holy Spirit so badly because once you got the Holy Spirit, you had access to all these other gifts too! The more time I spent in the prayer room, the clearer it became that I had the gift of knowledge, or what some people call a word of knowledge—the ability to discern information that you wouldn't normally have access to. That gift has helped me on countless bounty hunts. Sometimes God will give me a picture or an indication of something happening inside a person, and I know to ask them about that. The "how did you know?" look on their face confirms I heard right. Usually, I pray with them about it right there.

Don't get me wrong; the gift of knowledge is not some kind of psychic magic trick. It's a gift from the Holy Spirit that I have learned to listen to and heed, and He never took it away from me, even when I was wandering away from Him.

As an example of how God uses this gift in me, let me tell you a story. I was at the gym one day, and this guy who was about forty came up to me crying. He said, "Dog, please pray for my dad. He died last week. Why did God kill my dad? He was only sixty-one."

"Hang on, brother," I replied. "The Bible says the *thief* comes to steal, kill, and destroy.[8] I know it can be hard to understand, but God didn't kill your dad. He allowed it, that's true, and He doesn't always tell us His reasons why. Imagine, what if your dad had this little MG car and got into a wreck where he was so badly injured he had to have his limbs amputated and be put into the hospital to be fed through tubes? In that case, getting killed in the wreck would be an act of mercy."

The guy started shaking and crying, "Oh my God, Dog. How did you know that? Who told you that my dad had a little car?"

Nobody had told me. But when the young man approached me and showed me a photo of his dad, I felt the Lord remind me of an old MG car. It was a fleeting thought, just a quick image in my mind. I had never met this guy or his dad before, and I knew nothing about them.

"My dad had an old MG," the guy said, "and the family always told him, 'You're a crazy driver. You're gonna get in a wreck and die if you don't slow down.'"

"Man," I responded, "I am sorry you lost your dad. Really sorry. I can only tell you that when you showed me your dad's picture, the Lord showed me that car, brother. Maybe He allowed your dad to die in that crash to avoid a much worse existence here on earth. Maybe it was God's mercy."

That seemed to comfort him.

I can't even count the number of encounters I've had like that because God has given me a prophetic picture or impression. My mom was prophetic, as were my grandmother and great-grandmother. It was only natural for me to learn from Mom how to embrace these gifts and learn to use them. Some evenings she would have me sit next to her so we could study the Word of God together. She got me a dictionary so I could look up words in the Bible that I didn't understand. She also taught me how to use a concordance so I could look up the original Greek or Hebrew words. She impressed upon me the importance of reading the Bible in the context of the whole story. People come up with strange doctrines when they just pick out a verse here or there. So, as a boy, I loved God. I would even say that I was on fire for God.

That is—until I became a teenager. By the time I was thirteen or fourteen, all that started to change.

I've told you a lot about my mom and how she was basically a saint to me. She was patient and instructed me about right and wrong. I never questioned that she loved and accepted me.

Dad—Flash, as they called him, because he could run so

fast—was the complete opposite. My dad grew up with an abusive father who would tie him up by the wrists, securing him from the rafters of their barn, then beat him with a razor strap until he passed out. Harsh, excessive discipline is all he knew, and my dad applied that kind of parenting style to me. He would beat me with a one-inch-thick wooden paddle or belt buckle until I was completely black and blue, but he made sure to beat me where no one would see the marks peeking from under my shorts. Afterward, I couldn't sit down from the pain. One time, he gave me sixty-eight paddles in one session. I begged him to stop, but the more I cried, the more he beat me to try to toughen me up.

"I'm going to beat the savage out of you!" he often screamed as he lit my backside on fire.

My father hated when men cried. To him, it was a sign of weakness. Like all boys, I wanted his approval and affirmation, so as I got older, I would hold my breath to keep from crying. But then, he would beat me harder because he hadn't beaten me hard enough to make me cry. I just couldn't win!

Sometimes I would look back at his face while he whaled on me. So much anger there—he would grit his teeth, grinding his jaw.

"I gave you my name, boy!" he shouted. "Don't you understand?"

Of course I do, I thought. *You're my dad—of course you gave me your name.*

It just didn't make any sense.

I couldn't understand why Mom never tried to stop the beatings. Whenever my dad would start, she would walk out of the room, shut the door, and leave me alone with him. I know their thinking was "spare the rod, spoil the child," but I always wondered why my dad never beat any of his other kids like he beat me. Sometimes he did spank my sister Paula—usually when she would try to intercede on my behalf when my dad was out to whup me—but I still got the worst of it.

After it was all over and my dad cooled down, my mom would find me and try to offer some comfort. She would say things like, "In Psalms, it says that God keeps track of all your sorrows, son. He sees and knows everything. He has collected all your tears in a bottle. He has recorded every single one in a book."[9]

How does that help? I wondered. It was conflicting and confusing for one parent to tell me I should never cry and have the other one say that God collected all my tears in a bottle. All I knew was that I didn't like getting beaten. I honestly thought all fathers beat their sons like that. It wasn't until Jolene's revelation that I learned the reason behind why he targeted *me*.

After she told me Flash wasn't my real father, it made much more sense why he seemed to dislike me so much. Flash loved my mother. Even as a young boy, it was obvious to me that he loved her. So, if I wasn't his son, but he had agreed to give me his name on her behalf, I must have been a constant unpleasant reminder of a chapter in their life they probably wanted to forget. My dad never liked that my mother went to the reservation to minister either, and we never discussed it at home. He didn't like Indians, and it irritated him when I put feathers in a headband or gave a war whoop while playing.

As a kid, the more I went to church with my mom, the angrier Flash would get at me. If tears made you weak, religion made you weaker. He never said that to my mom, of course, but he always said it to me. One day, he heard me praying. He whipped around at me and spat out, "It's time you outgrow this faith crap. Praying is for sissies," and he backhanded me.

Dad constantly accused me of being weak and never seemed to run out of ways to toughen me up. One of his favorite ways was to make me fight other kids. If I didn't win a fight, he would beat me. If I brought home a bad grade, he would beat me. If it was Tuesday, he would beat me. He beat me at least three times a week for something—or nothing.

Finally, I started running away from home to avoid him. In fact, the first time I got arrested was because I'd run away from home. When the police brought me back home, my dad beat me. I ran away a dozen times or more before I finally left home for good. I was torn between being desperate to earn his approval and looking tough and wanting to be as far away from him as possible.

In sixth grade, a friend introduced me to sniffing airplane glue. The high from that made the physical and emotional pain of the beatings seem less. However, when my dad found out I was getting high from airplane glue, the beatings got even worse, making me want to escape even more by sniffing glue again. It was a vicious cycle. I stopped going to church, which broke my mom's heart and made her cry. But I was no longer torn between making my mom cry and wanting to make my dad proud—I was just angry.

That anger began the downward spiral into criminal activity. I dropped out during the seventh grade after suffering a particularly bad beating from my dad. I couldn't sit down at my desk because of the pain, so I stood through the class. My teacher got upset with me for standing and demanded to know why I wouldn't sit down. She wouldn't let up, and I was afraid if she sent me to the principal's office, they would call home, and Dad would beat me again.

Reluctantly, I showed her (and the class) my bruises. My teacher was horrified and sent me to the principal's office anyway—not because I was in trouble at school but because of the trouble at home. Some of the kids were quiet, but many smirked, and a few outright laughed at me. The words "Look how his dad beats him!" echoed in my head. Whether the words were said by other children or if they lived alone in my mind, I neither knew nor cared. I was humiliated.

"Duane," the principal asked as he studied my bruises, "did your father do this to you?"

I nodded my head yes, too embarrassed to speak up.

"I'm going to call your father," he announced.

"No, please don't!" I pleaded. "You'll only make him mad at me!"

He called to his secretary, "Bring me this boy's file; I want to place a call to his father."

"If you are going to call him, please ask him not to beat me like that anymore."

"It's going to be okay, son," he reassured me, dialing my dad. "Mr. Chapman, I have your son here in my office. Can you please come down here?"

It was only about thirty or forty minutes until my dad arrived, but it felt like an eternity. I was nauseated and sweating, and my legs were tired from standing because my butt hurt too much to sit down. I was dreading my father, worried about what he would do if the principal accused him of beating me.

My dad walked in all smiles.

"How can I help, sir? What has my boy done that's out of line?"

"Mr. Chapman, it looks to me like you might have given him

a pretty good whupping at home already. Listen, I know boys can get rowdy; as his father, you have every right to discipline him as you see fit. But perhaps you shouldn't discipline him with such force that other people can see the result. I suggest you don't leave marks next time."

I looked at the principal in disbelief. Flash's jaw was clenched, and when I got home, he added bruises on top of my bruises. I didn't go to school the next few days, and no one from the school bothered to check on me.

Looking back now, I think the principal probably meant to communicate that my dad shouldn't beat me so hard that he left bruises, but all I heard was, "Make sure you beat him where nobody sees the bruises." I was furious! I felt so betrayed.

Hatred built up inside me for the system. Probably for authority in general, now that I think about it. I hated the kids who teased me and the system that wouldn't protect me, so I dropped out. I left Rishel Junior High School shouting at my vice principal. Outside I jumped on my bike, flipped the bird at the school sign, and peeled off.

I never went back.

Shortly after, I started hanging out with gangs and bikers and soon became a prospect for the Devil's Diciples. My mom was horrified when she found out. I'm not sure if she was more upset that I was in a gang or because the word *devil* was in their name! I tried hard to explain that the group had nothing to do with Satan and was just a bunch of bad ass bikers, but she doubled down in her prayers for my soul.

I reassured my mother that I never once thought of myself as a disciple of the devil. And the whole time I was in their gang, I never stopped believing in God, even though my behavior was certainly far from Christian. Bikers accepted me. No one yelled at me, screamed at me, beat me, or told me what to do. I felt like I belonged, and soon I was going down a dark and dangerous road at high speed.

I had forgotten all about following God, but He hadn't forgotten about me.

TWO

BECOMING
DOG

You shall be called by a new name.

—Isaiah 62:2

I FIRST STARTED HANGING AROUND SOME OF THE DEVIL'S Diciples after I dropped out of school. Before I ever came to Phoenix, I had hung out with a Diciple named Tom-Tom. I got a fake ID that said I was eighteen so I could hang with him when I should've been in class. We got into trouble on a regular basis. One night while partying, we encountered a guy known as "Creature," who had the foulest mouth and nastiest temper I had ever seen. Seriously, if I had been standing next to him in a lightning storm, I would have moved as far from him as I could, certain the next bolt was for him because of the way He cursed God.

What really sealed the deal for me was when Creature flew into a rage at that party and turned a crucifix upside down, all while cursing God and calling Jesus a hippie. Now, I was definitely not hanging out in church anymore, and I was doing all kinds of things that I shouldn't have been doing—my list of sins was long—but I just could not take that kind of disrespect for God. Even drunk and crazy, I knew better than to mess with the Almighty!

So I challenged this giant man on the spot—got right in his face without even thinking about the consequences. The whole room got quiet.

I shouted, "God's wrath is real! You better be careful; it will rain down on your head for this kind of thing!"

I mean, I did everything but give an altar call—it was like all my childhood churchgoing was coming out gangster style.

Instead of jacking me into the wall, Creature took a step backward, fear in his eyes, stunned. Nobody moved.

"G-D Bible thumper!" Tom-Tom shouted as he put me into a playful headlock. The crowd went back to partying. "Duane the Bible thumper!" He laughed. "I'm gonna start calling you DOG . . . that's GOD spelled backward!"

From then on, I was Dog.

Tom-Tom and I made our way to Phoenix, where we joined up with a much larger group of Diciples. I didn't even have my colors yet, but I showed up anytime the club had business. One night we got the word, "All Diciples front and center." We were heading to the local Taco Bell to rip some patches (which meant stealing jackets from a rival gang). I was still just a prospect with a lot to prove, so I took a shot of whiskey, jumped on my hog, and showed up so full of rage that I was ready to fight anybody.

The Diciples were all there by the time the Dirty Dozen showed up and got off their bikes. Their sergeant at arms dismounted, cracked his knuckles loudly, and came forward. Behind him stood the members of his gang, arms folded, sizing us up. Our president, known as Hudat, said, "Get him, Dog!"

I'm the littlest guy here, I thought. *This guy could whip me! Why am I doing it? Why don't you send Little Pat?* (Little Pat was our sergeant at arms.)

Of course, I said none of this out loud. I just moved from where I was standing to face that giant and answer his challenge.

I was an amateur boxer, and I often boxed at Gringo's Graveyard. Members of the Diciples always bet on me because no one could outbox me. None of them had been trained in martial arts, so it didn't matter how big they were; I always knew right where to hit them to put them down. I assumed that was why Hudat picked me. I had earned a reputation for being fearless, and I worked hard to earn his respect. So anytime he called on me to fight, I fought with everything I had.

Hudat had a number of outstanding warrants, so he couldn't afford to get pulled over by the police—not even for a traffic ticket. We were riding together one afternoon when we pulled up to a stop sign. Riding without a helmet was a violation in Phoenix, so the cop took one look at us and flipped on his lights.

"I got this," I said to Hudat.

I flipped the cop the bird, shouted some expletives at him, and took off with Hudat right beside me. I let my Harley loose and heard the siren closing in behind me. I went down the down ramp, and Hudat went up the up ramp, but the cop followed me. I leaned into the wind and enjoyed the mixture of adrenaline and exhilaration I got every time a cop was in pursuit. I loved the thrill of the chase!

Hudat and I soon met up and continued to ride hard. I spotted a Blue Bird yellow school bus with an Assemblies of God sign painted on the side just ahead, sitting at the edge of a parking lot full of cars. I twisted the throttle, and we ripped around into the driveway, hid our bikes behind the bus, and sprinted inside the church. Somehow, we thought we couldn't be arrested if we were found inside a church—like when people claim sanctuary. Of course, we were wrong about this, but we assumed that if we made it into the building, then we were home free.

There was a church service in progress as we slipped into the back of the auditorium as quietly as we could, though we were out of breath from the chase, and we certainly drew some stares in our biker getup. We slid into the back row and listened hard to hear if that siren pulled into the church's parking lot. All of a sudden, someone near the front of the church started speaking loudly in tongues. A minute after he stopped, someone else stood up and delivered an interpretation of the tongues.

"What in the hell was that?" Hudat whispered to me. "Was that the devil?"

"Nah, brother," I answered, "he was just speaking in tongues. It's no big deal. I grew up in a church just like this."

Hudat shook his head and smiled at me.

"Tongues." He chuckled. "I'll be damned."

I was on good terms with Hudat. He knew me pretty well, so I didn't understand why I was still a prospect after being with the club for so long. Of course, most new recruits prospected for several months before they could become a member, but I felt like I had already earned my colors. Prospects had to hang around with the bikes and the "old ladies" whenever the Diciples went to a concert.

One night, Janice Joplin and Jimi Hendrix were playing, and I loved their music. I got fed up with sitting out in the parking lot. I wanted to go inside. Six or seven other prospects were hanging around, along with about a dozen women. I thought to myself, *I don't want to be standing out here with these punks. I want to be where the action is.*

"Where you going?" one of them questioned. "They gonna kill you for leaving the bikes!"

I shrugged my shoulders and said, "I'm going inside. You watch the bikes," then strutted away.

Once in the crowd, I made my way to the front. I noticed a group of guys wearing Hells Angels jackets—a sister club to the Diciples. I approached them, then sat down with the Hells Angels and started jamming out to the music. One of them asked a hippie sitting beside us if he could bum a swig off his wine bottle. Wanting to be tough and prove I could hang, I said, "Hey, give me a pull," I said, then I took a long drink. Pretty soon, someone dug out some weed and rolling papers.

"I'll do that for you," I said, and I rolled a couple of joints for them.

"How old are you, kid?" one asked.

"Eighteen," I lied.

Then I started smarting off about how much I hated being a prospect for the Diciples when I should already be a member. The wine and the weed made me a little too careless with my mouth. I made sure to slip out before the concert ended so I could be back with the bikes before the Diciples returned, certain I was in the clear. None of the other prospects would dare say a word. They were too afraid of me.

But I wasn't fast enough. They were all outside by their bikes when I returned. Their silence stopped me in my tracks. I had disrespected the whole gang. They rode away, leaving me standing there in the parking lot alone.

I'm done, I thought. *That's the end for me.*

The next morning, I was sound asleep when I was awakened by the unmistakable rumble of hogs rolling up outside. I was still rubbing the sleep out of the corners of my eyes when someone started pounding loudly on my door.

"Dog!" the voice said. "Open the door!"

I stumbled over and opened the door.

"Hey, man, what's going on? What's the problem?" I said.

"I hear you're the one with the problem," Hudat said. "I hear you got a problem with being a prospect. Is that right?"

Hudat and the guys pushed past me and came inside.

"Listen, brother; I'm the one you got throwing down with all those big guys—when Little Pat is *twice* my size. I'm the one getting you guys girls and putting myself in between you and the cops. Does that make me a prospect, or does that make me a Diciple?" I postured.

"Whine for us, Puppy," Little Pat said.

I gritted my teeth, but after what happened last night, this was not the time to confront him.

"Let me tell you something." Hudat squared his jaw and patted the patch on his jacket. "If I were to give you this patch and someone tried to snatch it from you, what would happen?"

"Well, give me your patch," I offered, "and no disrespect, but just try and take it away from me!"

"What did you just say to me?"

"I'm trying to tell you, brother, I ain't prospecting no more. I'm a Diciple, do you hear me? I'm a Diciple—a Devil's Diciple, forever and forever a Diciple!" I cried out.

Nobody said a word, waiting for what Hudat would do. Little Pat made for the door, and everybody followed him out—including me.

Hudat started grinning.

"All right, Dog, all right. Somebody give this punk his colors already!"

"What?" I exclaimed, amazed that I wasn't about to be beaten up by all the Diciples in my front yard. Little Pat motioned me over to him, reached into his saddle bag, and tossed me my jacket with the Devil's Diciples logo embroidered on the back. I slipped it on proudly.

"Come here—God-spelled-backward Dog. That ain't the only reason for your nickname, even though you *do* talk about God all the time!" he said, rolling his eyes.

That got laughter from everyone.

"Yeah, Dog should have been a preacher!" someone shouted.

"He ain't no dog," a guy nicknamed Indian called out. "He still ain't nothin' but a puppy!"

Now Indian had beat the crap out of me before, and I always hated that he refused to call me Dog. I couldn't stand for anyone to call me Puppy, and now that I had my colors, I wasn't going to let that go unchallenged!

"I ain't nobody's puppy!" I bristled, ready to fight Indian right there on the spot.

"Whoa there!" Hudat laughed. "You are not Puppy anymore— your name is *Dog*."

He looked at Indian and repeated, "Dog," which forever settled that. No one ever called me Puppy again.

"This Dog is man's best friend," he said and pointed at my chest. "Dogs are loyal. And you have never let this club down. Your name is now and forever Dog."

I thumped my jacket.

"I'm Dog Diciple!" I howled.

So I became a full-fledged Diciple—early. I wore the colors proudly and rode everywhere with my brothers.

———

I had very little contact with my mom and dad during those days. From time to time, I would call my mom, and she always asked me if I was going to church. Of course, I wasn't going to church, but I didn't want to disappoint her, so I'd do my best to make legitimate excuses. I know she saw right through them, but she never gave up on me.

After a few years, my parents decided to visit me in Arizona. I had told the Diciples stories about how mean my old man was, and I couldn't wait for them to meet him and finally have someone kick his butt. I told my biker brothers they would enjoy beating him up. I took my mom for a nice long walk, letting her know I wanted the chance to talk with her, leaving my dad alone with them. I kept my mom busy for about twenty minutes before turning around to walk back to my place with her.

I was already thinking up what I could say to her when we walked back and found Dad on the ground, but to my horror and surprise, they loved him! When we walked up, I found him hugging all my biker buddies and offering to barbeque for them. The next thing I knew, even Hudat was drinking beers with him!

All the guys kept coming over to me saying, "Man, your dad is the coolest guy."

They loved that my dad was tough; they couldn't get enough of him. What was I going to do? I had always wanted my dad to like me and be proud of me, but no matter what I did, he never seemed to approve. It seemed so odd that he was here, laughing it up with the motorcycle gang I'd run away from home to join.

As one of the youngest members, I was determined to prove myself as being the baddest, toughest Diciple there was. I tried my best to outdrink, outsmoke, and outfight everyone we came into contact with. We made a business out of stealing drugs from hippies and selling them. Very few people ever called the cops on us because most people neither liked nor trusted hippies, and no cop would ever believe a hippie who was stoned out of his mind anyway. It was an easy, pretty low-risk way to make money.

Sometimes, though, we did get caught, and I soon added robbery and drug charges to my growing police record. I kept on riding with the Diciples and accumulating more and more arrests until one near-fatal shootout made me think hard about the lifestyle I had chosen. I started losing interest in being a Diciple.

Looking back, I now think my mother's prayers were at work. She was always "praying a hedge of protection" around me, and I am sure she asked God every day for me to leave the Diciples. I didn't think about it then, but now I believe her prayers were what was making me restless.

All I knew was that I was just tired of proving myself twenty-four hours a day, seven days a week. I had created such a reputation for being a fighter. I fought constantly and was tired of taking all the punches so others could collect bets on me. On top of that, rolling hippies had always been easy money, but our last robbery ended with them shooting rifles at us from the roof—and one of them even pointed a pistol right in my face!

The idiot shot me! Well, shot at me. Thank God the bullet missed, but it grazed my scalp and took a piece of my mullet with it. My buddy Tim got hit badly and was bleeding so much I thought he would bleed out. Cops were everywhere.

I'm getting too old for this $#!%, I thought.

The paper dubbed it the "shootout on Mission Hill." I just know it was a turning point for me.

"I could be at the morgue right now," I said out loud to no one. I sat there a long time thinking about dying and death.

You didn't even think of Me, did you? I heard God say.

Oh my God, I thought. *I could have died, and I didn't even take two seconds to say, "Lord, forgive me for all my sins." I was so worried about dying. Worried about Tim losing blood. Worried about going to jail—I didn't even think about You, Jesus!*

That *really* shook me up. I left Phoenix, went back to Denver, and married the girl I had been dating for a while, LaFonda Sue Honeycutt. I was in love with her from the moment I first laid eyes on her, and I had gone back and forth from Denver to Phoenix for months to see her.

———————

The Vietnam War was in full swing. Several in the club were too old for the draft, and like most outlaw clubs formed after World War II, there was a strong tie of loyalty to veterans. We were patriots. We might have committed crimes, but we had a code among us, a sort of honor among thieves that we held to. My dad had also served in the navy, and I wanted to do my bit, so I went to the local recruiter's office to sign up for military service. I passed the initial recruitment test, but when it came time to fill out my arrest history on the application, I had to ask for an extra piece of paper.

I thought juvenile records were sealed, but apparently not from the military. You are supposed to put down *everything*. I thought it would be okay because I had heard you could sign a moral waiver and still serve as long as you didn't lie on your application. But when the recruiter saw my list, he said, "Son, the military would rather take women and children before they take the likes of you. You are 4-F. Do you know what that means? You are unfit for military service." And with that, he showed me to the door.

I was disappointed. Even angry. I didn't want to tell my dad and give him another reason not to be proud of me. Ultimately, I decided it was no skin off my back. If the military didn't want me, I didn't want them either. I wasn't in the Diciples anymore, but when the military rejected me, I went right back to what I knew—robbing and stealing.

That shootout on Mission Hill was heavy on my mind the day my son was born. Having a baby then wasn't like it is now. Dads had to sit out in a waiting room until it was all over. I will never forget the feeling when they handed this little spider monkey—all arms and legs—to me. Love rushed through me. And pride. All I wanted to do was protect that little man.

At last, I had a son, and I wanted to give him my name. I didn't want him to be a junior either. "Duane Lee Chapman II," I announced to the nurse. "That's his name!"

Three days later, we were allowed to take him home. They brought a wheelchair for LaFonda, and after they settled her into it, they handed the baby to her.

"I'll take him," I told the nurse.

"I'm sorry," she said, "the mother carries the baby out of the hospital."

"Not this time," I protested. I grabbed my son and held him close as I walked beside LaFonda while the nurse wheeled her outside. Once we got home, I sat there holding him, touching his little hands and feet—five fingers and five toes on each. I cradled his small head, and I marveled at how perfect and tiny his features were.

Thank You, God, I prayed, tears streaming down my face. *Thank You for giving me this perfect little boy.*

That's it, I decided. *No more felonies.*

I didn't want to leave Duane Lee without a father. I told myself I was not going to go to prison and let my boy grow up calling someone else Daddy. I decided it was time to seek out a legitimate job.

I became a vacuum salesman, which, it turned out, I was pretty good at. I had a knack for talking to people and selling things. I soon became one of the highest-earning salesmen at the company, but I still liked the thrill of the outlaw life. It was a constant battle between wanting to walk the straight and narrow and make something of myself and wanting to be the bad boy. Even though I was no longer part of the Diciples, I still liked hanging around with bikers, drinking in bars, and smoking weed. When our second son, Leland, was born, I redoubled my efforts to be a better man, but I made no shortage of bad decisions.

My heart always seemed to be in the right place, even if my head wasn't.

Sometimes when I meet people now, they ask me if I feel like the Prodigal Son—you know, the one who left his home, squandered his inheritance, then came back with nothing and was received with love and forgiveness by his father.[1] I can understand why others might think that story fits. But I can honestly say that I have never felt like the Prodigal Son. Even when I was in the middle of making the worst possible choices and making terrible mistakes, I never really felt like I was running away from God. I always knew He was there. I always knew He was with me.

I think I relate more to King David in the Bible. David was the youngest son of Jesse—the boy they thought was least likely to make anything of himself. But David had proven himself in his youth by fighting a lion and a bear to protect his father's sheep.

When David's older brothers were all serving in the army, and all of Israel was too afraid to face down their enemy Goliath, David bravely stood up and brought the giant down with just a slingshot and a few stones. He was a scrapper, like me. His skill as a fighter made him popular and gave him great favor with King Saul, but eventually (like me), David became an outlaw. He was kind of like an ancient Robin Hood for a while, living in the desert among a company of bandits known as his "mighty men."

But all throughout his life, David loved God. When he was a boy tending sheep, he wrote and sang psalms. Then God empowered him to kill the bear, the lion, and Goliath. Later in life, when he fought glorious battles and became famous and everybody knew his name, it was still God who protected him every time. And when David did really terrible things—like sleep with Bathsheba and send her husband to the front lines to be killed so David could have her to himself and hide his sin—he always turned back to God and repented of his sins.

Again and again, David's character showed flaws, but then he did great exploits. He was known as a man after God's own heart[2]—even when he sinned publicly, everyone knew he loved God. The Bible records that God had a special affection for David. No matter what, God's hand of protection, favor, and blessing was always on David.

I feel the same way. No matter what, God's hand has always been on me.

When David was just a boy, Samuel had prophesied over him that he would be king, then Samuel anointed David with oil and consecrated him to that service. I can relate to that too. The prayers my mother prayed over me as a small boy served as a divine preservative in my life. My mother, my grandmother, and even my great-grandmother spoke words over me and never ceased reminding me of who I was and who God was to me.

It was prophesied over me several times that I would preach the gospel and speak to millions. Like David, I was also anointed with oil and consecrated for God's service. No matter where I have gone or what I have done, those early prayers have always drawn me right back to where I started.

As I held baby Leland, memories flooded me. I thought about Grandpa Mike and how he was always there to teach me how to do things, how he listened to me and spent time with me. I thought about how my mother taught me right from wrong. I thought about how she took me to church, taught me how to pray and sing, and brought me to minister with her on the Indian reservation. And though she and Grandpa Mike didn't really use the word *destiny* very often, they certainly made it clear that I had been bought with a price and that my life was not my own. I belonged to God.

I wanted so badly to be a good father—the kind of father that my dad was not. The kind of father that Grandpa Mike must have been to my mother. I wanted to be there for my sons, and I vowed never to lay a hand on them like my dad had beaten me.

I was excited to be a dad, and I made a promise to God that I would never join another biker gang or go back to jail. For the first time, I had a good job and something to live for. It felt like I had a fresh start, and life finally seemed to be on the up and up. I had no idea that destiny was chasing me and that I was about to face the greatest challenge of my life.

THREE

CAGED
DOG

The Lord was with him; he showed him kindness and granted him favor in the eyes of the prison warden. So the warden put Joseph in charge of all those held in the prison, and he was made responsible for all that was done there.

—Genesis 39:21–23 NIV

I WOKE UP IN A COLD SWEAT. MY HEART WAS RACING—IT WAS so real. I dreamed that I had plowed into the back of a car on my chopper. I saw it coming, but I couldn't stop. I ran into it at full speed. Then, I saw my mangled hog lying on the highway, mirror ripped off, tires in the air. I saw paramedics zipping up a body bag, red and blue lights flashing in slow motion, reflecting in water on the pavement. I didn't hear any sound; it was like I was watching a movie with the volume turned off. But there was no mistaking that it was me in that bag.

"You better straighten up," Rick Ivy (a.k.a. Poison Ivy) had told me earlier that day from a pay phone.

"I know," I answered him. "I know I gotta get my act together."

But I shook off his warning too.

The next evening, my buddy Donny called. I was still hanging out with some of the Diciples even though I'd promised God I wouldn't.

"Want to go coyote hunting?" he asked.

"Yeah, sure. Come pick me up," I answered. I loved tracking things.

"Dog, don't go," LaFonda said.

"Why not?" I asked her.

"I wouldn't go." She shook her head and said, "Something's wrong."

LaFonda had great intuition. I find women, in general, have a gift of intuitiveness. More so than men. I wish I had been smart enough to take LaFonda seriously when she told me she had a bad feeling something was going to happen that night. I wish I had taken that dream more seriously when she warned me not to go out with my buddies, but I didn't listen.

On September 16, 1976, I grabbed my .308 rifle and my coyote caller—that's a little thing you blow into that sounds like a rabbit or some small animal in distress. It attracts the coyotes to come to find the source of the sound. Donny Kurkendall pulled up, and I took my stuff and jumped in the car with him, Ruben Garza, and Cheryl Fisher. They were already pretty drunk and seemed much more interested in getting high than going hunting.

"Let's just go to the woods, Donny," I said.

He polished off some Mad Dog and said, "I need a joint, brother!"

We drove around trying to score some pot, but we would have had better luck finding a nun inside a strip club than we did finding marijuana that night.

"Hey," one of them said, "let's try Jerry Lee. I bet he's got a stash!"

"Come on, man, let's just go the woods. Leave Jerry Lee alone."

Jerry Lee Oliver was my friend, and I wanted no part in robbing him. Besides, he had a mean temper. It just wasn't a good idea.

Donny pulled into a gas station and filled up the car with gas while Ruben went in to buy beer. I didn't even get out of the car. When everyone was back in the car, Donny revved the engine and sped off to Jerry's place. I was standing outside of the car with Cheryl when a shot rang out, followed by Donny running outside screaming.

"What happened?" I shouted. "Did Jerry shoot you?"

"His shoulder," Donny panted. "I only shot him in the shoulder!"

"You what?!" I said. "What did you do? Is he dead?"

"No, man, I only grazed him; get in the car!" Donny screamed.

"I need to check on Jerry Lee!" I shouted as Cheryl slid behind the wheel.

"Get in the car!" Cheryl yelled. "Donny needs a doctor!"

I still thought Jerry had shot Donny; I didn't know Donny's hand was bleeding because shrapnel from his three-piece shotgun had exploded in his hand—Donny's blood was from his own shrapnel. After we dumped Donny at the hospital, Cheryl dropped me off at my house. Once inside, I called 911 and told the operator to send an ambulance to Jerry's house. When LaFonda overheard my call, she was alarmed and angry.

"I told you not to go!" she screamed at me.

"But I didn't do anything wrong, baby!" I defended myself. "I didn't even know Donny took his gun in there. I thought he was just trying to buy some pot! Oh my God, Donny shot Jerry in the shoulder! I had to call 911. Somebody has to check on Jerry Lee!"

"Where were you when it happened?" LaFonda asked, shaking; she was so angry.

"Outside," I answered. "I didn't even go in the house; the boys just went inside to get some pot. I was outside the whole time, then I heard a gun go off, and then Donny ran outside bleeding!"

I didn't realize I had not hung up with the 911 operator when I confessed to being at the scene—even though I hadn't pulled the trigger.

"I have to go, baby," I said. "I have to make sure Jerry Lee is okay." I jumped on my Harley and took off for his house.

When I arrived, medics were already on the scene and

wheeling Jerry out on a stretcher while the Pampa police questioned him about who had shot him. Jerry told them it was one of the Devil's Diciples, but I heard him tell Officer Love I was not the shooter.

He said, "Dog didn't do it," so I thought I would be okay.

The next morning, however, we woke up to the news announcing that I was wanted in connection with Jerry's murder.

"Murder!" I said in disbelief. "Oh my God, Jerry's dead!"

I froze. I couldn't move. But then the reality of being arrested for his murder sent a rush of adrenaline through me, and I was on my feet in a second. I shoved some things into a bag and told LaFonda to get the kids and meet me on the highway; we would run to Colorado.

"We'll go to my mom's," I said, but before I could finish my sentence, there was a knock at the door. I panicked. "Tell them I'm at work!" I mouthed.

LaFonda answered the door, and I heard her say as cool as a cucumber, "No, Officer, Duane's not at home right now; he already left for work."

Of course, my truck was parked in the driveway; I had obviously not already left for work. I heard one siren, then two. I bolted to—and through—the back door, ripping it off the hinges. I ran across my yard, jumped my neighbor's fence, and scrambled into the alley, certain the cops were right behind me. But there, at the end of the alley, was a police cruiser. I was trapped. The guy who would one day be famous as a bounty hunter for bringing in hard-to-catch fugitives had just been caught in an embarrassingly short time. There was no real chase.

Pampa, Texas, is a small town, and I'd had many previous run-ins with the police, so they knew my name and my face.

"You're going down, Chapman," one smirked while the other put me in cuffs. I took the right to remain silent seriously, and I said nothing on the ride to the station.

By the end of the day, Donny, Cheryl, Ruben, and I were all in custody—charged with first-degree murder.

The judge set my bail at $50,000. *Fifty thousand dollars*, I thought. *Why not make it a million?*

There was no way I could come up with that kind of money, so I sat in jail, getting angrier and angrier. I fought with everybody they put in a cell with me until they finally had to put me in solitary confinement. That cell had a little mailbox slot you could open up to talk through or pass in food.

I got a visit from Rev. Gerald Middaugh from the Pampa Assemblies of God. He tried to talk to me, but I was angry and had no interest in a conversation with him. Through the slot, he noticed a copy of *The Cross and the Switchblade* lying on my bunk.

"Did you ever read that book?" he asked.

"No, man," I answered, "my mom gave me a copy after I joined the Diciples, but I ain't never read it, and I don't intend to."

"Maybe you should," he encouraged. "It's about a man named Nicky Cruz, who was once a member of the Mau Maus. He was in a gang just like you, and his friend died too. You don't have much to do in there; maybe you should try reading it to pass the time."

I shrugged. Talking about the book made me think of my mom, and I knew she was really upset that I was in there. Reverend Middaugh took my silence as an opening. "Or you could read the Bible . . ."

That just made me mad, though, so I said, "Unless you are

here to post my $50,000 bail, you can just move along. I'll use your Bible to roll joints!"

He remained calm. "Jesus loves you, Duane," he said.

"My name is Dog," I answered.

"Well, Jesus loves you, Dog, and if you want God to reduce your bail, you'll have to ask Him. The Bible says, 'Ask, and ye shall receive.' Why not ask God for a bail reduction and see what happens?"

"Listen, preacher," I said, "let me come straight with you. I am already a Christian. I grew up in church. God even warned me in a dream that if I didn't straighten up, something bad was going to happen, and I guess this is it. But don't you worry about me. I wasn't even in that house and had nothing to do with that murder, so I will be okay. I will be a Christian when I get out of here."

The reverend left, and before too many days inside, I figured out how to work the system. I got really bad headaches, and I needed stronger drugs than the Tylenol they gave me—and they were not that hard to come by. Truthfully, you can get anything inside if you know how. When LaFonda visited, she brought me Fiorinal . . . *and* a Bible. The drugs were to keep me from acting so violent and crazy, and I guess she hoped the Bible might help me turn my life around.

Boredom and frustration were what finally made me open it and read. Memories of my mom and aunt flooded me. I thought about the prophecies spoken over me in church, and I remembered giving testimonies and felt something tugging on me. I considered myself a "good" bad guy. I only stole drugs from people who sold them to children. Yeah, I liked to party too much, and I too easily hooked up with women, but I didn't consider myself to be a bad man—just a good man who did bad things.

I hated that I was in prison. I was mad at myself for LaFonda and the boys not having me around, and right then and there, I repented.

God, forgive me, I prayed. *I'm sorry for all the bad things I've done, and I want to live on the straight and narrow. You helped me get the sixty dollars I needed as a kid and gave me a horse when I asked You for one. Will You help me now and reduce my bail? I'll stop running with the Diciples. I'll stop cheating on LaFonda. I'll be a better dad . . .* and on and on I went with promises God knew I would not keep. But He answered my prayer anyway—like He always does.

Forty-eight hours later, the judge set my bail at just $5,000! I couldn't believe it! Grandpa Mike paid a bondsman $500 to get me out of jail, and when he took me to his office, a huge man was standing behind the bail bondsman's desk, wearing an eye patch. This guy had muscles on his muscles.

"Ever hear of a bounty hunter?" the bondsman asked.

I shook my head no.

"Well, if you run, I'm gonna send this guy after you," he said, pointing to the huge man with the eye patch.

Now that I was out, I needed work. Before the arrest, I had a job driving parts to oil fields when I wasn't running with bikers. But I worked there with Donny and some of the other Diciples, and I knew if I was going to change my life, I better not go back to the same crowd.

I remembered Reverend Middaugh had asked me what I would do when I got out. "Well, where will you go? Where will you work?" he had asked.

So I gave him a call.

"We need a janitor at our church," he said. "Why not come meet me over here?"

The reverend showed me all around the building, showed me what he wanted me to clean, and then he handed me the keys to the church.

"You're giving me the keys?" Surprised, I asked, "You know I'm a convict, right?"

He laughed. "God watches this building, son. It's His church, not mine."

So I started showing up to clean the church. I brought my tape recorder with me to play music while I worked, and I found some cassettes with songs I used to sing with my mom. I went back to the sound booth, turned it on, then put one microphone in front of the tape recorder while I sang into the other one. No one was there, but I sang my heart out. I cried. I prayed. And I sang. My mama would have been proud!

Everyone in the congregation knew I was out on bail for a murder charge, but I have to admit, they were pretty accepting. That Sunday, Reverend Middaugh said, "Duane here has a testimony he wants to share," and he pointed at me.

"I do?" I asked, surprised.

"You do," he answered. "Come on up here and tell us about what God did for you."

When I shared my testimony and how God had been at work to reduce my bail and release me from prison, the response from people was amazing. They shook my hand and slapped me on the back, and many said, "You should be a preacher!"

Reverend Middaugh sent me to Lubbock to share my testimony at Sydney Love's church. I sat in the back, and no one knew me. Pastor Love gave an altar call, and this big biker got out of his seat and started walking down the aisle. I jumped up right behind him and followed him all the way there. I knelt next to him, and the church elders went down the line praying for us one by one.

This eighty-five-year-old lady came down the row. My mom would say she was an "elder lady of Zion." She touched me on the head to pray, and when she did, she jumped back and started saying, "Thank You, God. Thank God, this young man has been called to the ministry! He will lead millions of children to the Lord."

It was just like when I was a child. Even now, with all the bad things I had done, it seemed like God wasn't finished with me. He had called me when I was a boy, and I couldn't escape Him. I started sharing my "killer testimony" in churches, and to my surprise, when I would give my version of an altar call, people always came forward. Every single time, I felt God. I was always really moved when people responded to Jesus.

After that, LaFonda and I started going to church every Sunday. I sold my Harley Panhead—man, I loved that bike—and with that sale, I felt like I had closed the chapter on my biker days. Word started to get around that "Dog was on the Jesus wagon now," which helped me keep my nose clean while I waited for the hearing, all the while praying God would let the judge show mercy.

A year later, I was called before the court and found guilty of first-degree murder, but the judge did show me mercy. In Texas, if you were present when the crime was committed, you were guilty of the crime. I could have been sentenced for up to ninety-nine years, but the judge gave me five. God answered my prayer for mercy.

Still, five years at the Huntsville Unit (Texas State Penitentiary at Huntsville) was serious. Huntsville was a hard-labor prison. Five years in Huntsville felt like a life sentence at the time.

I had a hard time processing the sentence. It was a long, degrading trip to Huntsville. Once there, they stripped you naked with sixty other guys, gave you a number, and put you in a holding cell. I was no longer Dog or even Duane; I was Prisoner #271097. What do you think was inside that cell? Two books: a Gideons Bible and *The Cross and the Switchblade*.

I broke down and said, *Lord, I didn't do this! You know I didn't kill that man!*

You didn't do this, God answered, *but look around you. Every brick in this prison is built on a crime you committed.* That's *why you're here: to pay for your crimes. I will not be mocked. Whatever a man soweth, that shall he also reap.*

Oh my God, I repented again. *Oh my God, I'm so sorry. I repent. I'll count the bricks, and I'll repent for every single sin.*

I opened that Gideons Bible, closed my eyes, and just pointed my finger at a verse. My mother always told me not to do it that way because what if I pointed to the verse in Matthew about Judas where he "went and hanged himself"?[1] But that day the Bible fell open to the book of John, and the verse I pointed at said, "Lovest thou me? . . . Feed my sheep."[2]

Just then, outside my cell, there was a line of guys being rounded up, and one of them said, "Bah-ah-ah-ah-ah! They're herding us up like a bunch of sheep!"

"Davy, it's cattle!" I shouted. "It's supposed to be a bunch of cattle, not sheep."

Sheep. "Feed My sheep," the Bible said. Then it dawned on me. *I'm here to help them; I am in this prison right now to help these guys. They are God's sheep!*

The wardens took pleasure in inflicting new methods of pain and suffering on the inmates, and the inmates were no better. Prison brings out the worst in men. It is survival of the fittest, and you quickly learn to keep your head down and your mouth shut. Dominance and hierarchy are established through violence; if you show the slightest sign of weakness, you will be targeted and violated.

I learned quickly that if you prayed or carried a Bible or a cross, that put a target on your back. Religion was seen as weakness. So I believed while I was in there I was supposed to be a sort of prison preacher, but I also knew if I wasn't going to get killed, I had to do it prison style, not like any Assemblies of God church I had been in.

I didn't pretend I was a perfect, sanctified saint of any kind. I was in prison. I talked like I was in prison. I fought like I was in prison. Some days just being inside the joint was enough to make me crazy. I really had issues with wanting women; that's a battle I have fought most of my life.

Prisoners in Huntsville did hard labor every single day. We got beaten up by the guards. Eventually, I learned how to get on their good side. I went to the prison chapel to pray. I knew God was with me every single day. He told me He would never turn against me, and I knew it was true.

I went from working in the fields to being the laundry bookkeeper. Eventually, I got the chance to become the warden's barber. That's an incredible story, and you can find that one, along with many of my other prison stories, in my first book, *You Can Run but You Can't Hide.*

On Mother's Day, a bunch of moms came out to see their sons in prison. My mother wasn't there, but the warden asked me to do the Mother's Day prayer at the service they held. Basically, he gave me the message to "stick with the script," and he handed me a paper with the prayer I was supposed to pray written down. When it was time for me to pray, I put the piece of paper off to the side and just spoke from my heart.

"All you mothers out there," I began, "you know people can say anything to us about our dads. They can say anything about us or even our kids, but nobody is allowed to say *anything* about our moms. Moms are special people. And look around; every one of us here is sorry that we put you through this. We are ashamed that you have to come here to prison to visit us . . ."

I kept on talking for a few minutes. Then I led a prayer that started by asking God to forgive us for the sins we committed and ended with, "so may God bless all our mamas in Jesus' name, amen." Most of the moms were crying, and most of the men were too—except for the warden. He looked stern.

Not many days after that, Warden Horton walked up and said, "My office." I was nervous, and when I went to his office, two other guys were sitting outside, waiting ahead of me to see the warden. One of them was really depressed. He started talking about wanting to kill himself, and he meant it. I could see it in his eyes. I believed he was going to do it.

Prisoners never ask each other what they are in for, but it's okay to ask, "How much time you got left?" So that's how I started up a conversation with him.

"Two years," he answered.

"Brother, listen, you can make it two years. I've got five years," I said.

In prison, you didn't say, "Would you like to ask Jesus to come into your heart?" So instead, I looked him in the eyes and said, "You understand about Jesus, right?"

He shook his head yes.

"And you know He died for us, right? That He died for our crimes, and He loves us?"

Again, he shook his head yes.

"God loves you, brother. So let's not be thinking about ending your life anymore. You've got something to live for, you understand me?"

That's how it was. There was no "Close your eyes and bow your head," like they do in a church service, but I had no problem talking about Jesus being the Son of God or that the Holy Spirit came down and planted a seed in Mary . . . lots of guys in there got saved—just not at an altar.

This prisoner looked at me, and I saw his eyes change. I knew he wasn't going to kill himself anymore. We fist-bumped, and he said, "Thanks, man."

I didn't know the warden had been listening.

"You fancy yourself some kind of prison counselor?" the warden asked me when we got inside his office.

"No, sir," I said. "I just know I like to help some of these guys, and they like to tell me about their problems."

From then on, when somebody inside would get bad news from the outside, the warden gave me a chance to talk with them about it. I became the unofficial inmate counselor. I have always liked helping people, and I shared a gangster God while in prison to reach the gangsters for God. I prayed over my food in front of them, and most of them learned that my nickname came from *God*, spelled backward. Everyone in the joint knew I was on the "Jesus wagon."

People often ask me how the backseat prison ministry I became famous for on *Dog the Bounty Hunter* started. I tell them, "It began at the Huntsville Unit, ministering to the inmates."

FOUR

RELEASED
DOG

At last we have freedom, for Christ has set us free! We must always cherish this truth and firmly refuse to go back into the bondage of our past.

—Galatians 5:1 TPT

WHEN I WAS FIRST SENT TO THE HUNTSVILLE UNIT, IT WAS still segregated. Black men were put in cells with each other on one side of the prison, and White men were put on the other side. The prison began to integrate the population while I was serving my time, but guards did not treat Black people and White people the same. Guards were rough on all inmates, but Black prisoners got worse treatment across the board.

There was no privacy in prison. The guards screened every letter received before a prisoner got to read it. Usually, inmates were given bad news from home privately. I don't believe that was meant to be a courtesy; it was more for safety. When a prisoner got that kind of letter, it wasn't uncommon for them to be put into solitary confinement temporarily to protect them from hurting themselves, hurting others, or trying to escape to get to their loved ones.

As the unofficial prison counselor, I was generally allowed to pay them a visit in solitary and talk with them. I was a good listener, and I had a gift for calming people down, offering comfort, and getting them to see things from a new perspective and accept the situation.

One morning on my way to work at the prison barbershop, prisoners were lined up as usual for mail call. Standing there in line was Bigfoot—a large Black man who got his nickname because he wore a size 16 shoe! He was unmistakable in any crowd; you couldn't miss him. A few guards were there as all the letters were passed out.

One of the guards said, "All inmates whose mothers are still alive, take one step forward."

Most of the guys took the step, expecting they were about to get a letter from their mom. But one guard, who was especially cruel to Black inmates, sneered and said, "Hey, not so fast, Bigfoot. You step out of the line."

His meaning was clear. Every guy in the joint immediately knew that Bigfoot's mother was dead, but before the guards could make it down the line to pull him aside, Bigfoot went crazy! He screamed in disbelief mixed with rage, and his eyes looked wild. Espinoza, a boss inside the prison, grabbed him by the arm and tried to drag him away from the other inmates, but Bigfoot easily tossed him to the side and bolted. Espinoza was no match for Bigfoot, and in three giant steps, Bigfoot was running at full speed, headed for the creek to make a break for it.

Everyone started shouting at him to stop, knowing what would happen next—a prisoner caught trying to escape could be shot. It was chaos, with guards and inmates all yelling. Big Lou (as we called Lt. Hillegeist) drew his weapon, aimed right at Bigfoot, and screamed, "Stop, or I'll shoot!"

In a split second, before I even had a chance to think about it, I ran after Bigfoot, shouting back over my shoulder, "Don't do it, Big Lou!"

As my friend Ronnie and I chased him down, I was waiting for a shot to go off, and I was now directly in between Big Lou and Bigfoot. I expected a bullet to rip through my body at any moment—I think I even heard him cock his .38! Ronnie tackled Bigfoot from behind, which slowed him down but didn't make him stop. I was on him the next second, and when Ronnie pushed him to the ground on his stomach, I grabbed his arms and held them behind his back.

"Calm down, man, calm down," I said, "you're gonna get yourself killed!"

Big Lou ran up panting, with his gun still in his hand. He stuffed it back into its holster and tossed me his handcuffs, saying, "Cuff him up, bounty hunter."

Bounty hunter? What? I thought and clicked the cuffs around Bigfoot's big wrists. We all walked back to the yard together, but now Ronnie and I had a new problem. The yard was quiet—too quiet. We were met with cold, hard, angry stares because it looked like Ronnie and I were in on it with the guards—rats. This put our lives so much in danger that the warden informed us we would have to be transferred right away.

I pleaded with Warden Horton. "Give us a chance to talk to the guys. We can straighten this out."

That night in the yard, it was hostile. We knew we didn't have much time, so we approached the right group—the toughest guys inside with the most ruthless reputation.

"Listen," I said, "I don't know what you've heard, but the guards told Bigfoot in front of everybody that his mama was dead. They singled him out to humiliate him, to mock him. That's why he went crazy, and when he ran for the creek, they were going to shoot him."

We made it plain that Ronnie and I had played no part in what the guards did to harass Bigfoot.

"We ran after him to protect him, *to save his life*, not to rat him out or get him tossed in solitary," I explained.

Thank God they believed me and spread the word. Not only did

I stop getting threats but inmates also started leaving gifts outside my cell—things like coffee, cigarettes, and candy—the kind of stuff I could get in trouble for.

Big Lou pulled me aside, and I was sure he was about to let the hammer down on me for getting in between him and Bigfoot. Contraband was all the excuse he needed to make my life miserable. But instead, he looked me in the eyes and said, "Well, *Dog the Bounty Hunter*, your bread's been buttered."

There it was again, *bounty hunter*. That was the second time he had called me that. The image of the giant Indian with the eye patch at the bail bond office flashed in my head. I still had no idea what a bounty hunter did, but I liked the sound of it.

"Dog the Bounty Hunter." I tried it out.

The seed had been planted. I started reading books in the library and looking up information about what bounty hunters were, what they did, and how they got paid. It seemed like all the bounty hunters I read about started out as felons, then something happened to them while they were in prison, and they turned their lives around and became good guys. I felt like I was reading about my future. I wanted to be a good guy all the time from now on, and I knew I could do it.

The nickname "Dog the Bounty Hunter" started to stick. Just like people spoke prophetic words over me when I was a boy that I would be a preacher one day, now people were saying words over me that I would be a bounty hunter. I am sure none of them thought of it as a prophecy—I certainly didn't—but words spoken out loud have power. Incredible power.

Who knew then that the prophecies spoken over me in my childhood about ministering to millions would be connected to a career as a bounty hunter, or that such a career would give me the opportunity to be in front of millions of people? God works in mysterious ways!

But I couldn't become a bounty hunter while I was an inmate. When I counted those prison bricks that afternoon, I told God I would tell people about Him and not be ashamed. I started writing letters to request Bibles for inmates, and so many were delivered to me that the guards grew suspicious and wanted to know what I was doing with all those Bibles.

"I'm giving them away," was all I said.

The weirdest thing is that the guys I gave them to wanted me to sign them. At night I sometimes had a pile of them in my cell. I would write their name and sign it "From Dog the Bounty Hunter." I prayed over those Bibles and said, *Lord, I know You love these guys. Help them to find You inside the pages of this book like I did.*

When I was a kid, my mom taught me the story of Joseph from the Old Testament. God used a prison sentence to prepare Joseph to step into his destiny. Joseph had gifts. He could interpret dreams, and he was a leader. His time in prison landed him a job inside Pharaoh's house. That job turned out to be how God used Joseph to save his own people from starving in a famine.

If Joseph had never gone to prison, he never would have had the chance to save his family. God did the same kind of thing for me. I'm not saying God sent me to prison; I'm the one who chose crime, and I was the one in that car the night of Jerry Lee Oliver's murder. But God used my prison sentence to set me up to step into my destiny too. He worked it for my good, just like the Bible promised. I went into prison as Dog Diciple; I came out of prison as Dog the Bounty Hunter.

God had a plan for me I couldn't mess up.

And it's a good thing, too, because I certainly tried.

———————

Shortly before my release date, I got a blow I didn't see coming. LaFonda wrote to me in prison to tell me that she'd been having an affair with my best friend, Jim Darnell—the man I had asked to look after her while I was in the joint. She divorced me not long after I was inside, which devastated me then, but I always believed we would get back together once I was out of prison. This letter said she and Jim had fallen in love, and she planned to marry him and take Duane Lee Jr. and Leland with her.

All my goals of living a good, honest life when I got out of prison flew out the window. I was consumed with rage and revenge. I wanted to kill Jim. The wardens tried to counsel me and warn me not to do anything stupid, or I'd find myself back in Huntsville for good.

I didn't care.

"Hold my cell for me—cell 11 is mine," I told the warden. "Don't give it to nobody until I get back!"

When I was released and walked out of that prison, I fully intended to kill Jim Darnell and be right back inside Huntsville. I heard the voice of God trying to warn me off my warpath, but I was too angry, and I felt betrayed. I still loved LaFonda, and I had been dreaming about our life together once I got back home. I couldn't believe my best friend would steal my wife and my boys! All I could think about was sending him to heaven—or hell;

I really didn't care which at that moment. I would stop at nothing until he was dead.

I left prison wearing the same clothes I wore when I got arrested. I had a check in my pocket from the prison for $200 and every intention of being back inside within the week. Thank God, in His mercy, He found ways to derail my stupidity.

I cashed the check, wasted some of the money on a woman, then bought a gun (illegally) and a one-way plane ticket back to Colorado. This was well before 9/11, so security was nothing like it is today. Still, you weren't supposed to take a weapon with you. They had metal detectors, and if I had gotten caught, I would have been arrested on the spot—especially with fresh parole papers in my pocket! I bluffed my way through the lax security at the airport entry with a gun stuffed in my pants. I walked to my gate as confidently as if I was a security officer and boarded the airplane.

Once on board, I was miserable. I sat down in the back of the plane on the aisle in the very last row. There was a battle between the angels and the demons going on inside my head. One was telling me God had a plan for me, and this was not it; the other was telling me to go kill the lousy betraying scum who had once been my friend! I wanted to—I needed to—drown the voices out.

I had not touched alcohol in over two years, but when the flight attendant walked by with her cart, I ordered two of those tiny airplane bottles of vodka. Then two more, all of which I drank down in less than fifteen minutes. That much alcohol in a clean system meant I got drunk fast, but I felt less angry. I leaned my head back and closed my eyes for a minute, and when I opened them, I noticed this tall, fair-skinned, redheaded man sitting in my row next to the airplane's window.

Back when I boxed, I always hated fighting redheads.

I was also made fun of in school by a couple of redheads when I was a kid. So I stayed away from people with red hair in general. Whenever I boxed a guy with red hair, he always seemed to have some kind of extra-fiery temper that made him quick and indestructible. When I saw this redhead sitting next to me, I thought, *No, man, not today. Who is this guy?*

The beverage service was over, but I could just lean over my chair and talk to the flight attendants because I was in the back of the plane.

"Hey, miss, can I get another one of these?" I asked, holding up the tiny vodka bottle. That would have been my fifth.

But the attendant pretended she didn't hear me (she probably thought I had already had enough), and the redheaded man placed his hand on my arm and asked me where I was going. I told him I was on my way back to Colorado to hunt down and kill the man who stole my wife.

"You are?" he asked. "How are you planning to do that?"

"With this."

I leaned forward and lifted my shirt, showing him the butt of my gun, thinking that would shut him up. He was completely unfazed. He didn't even seem concerned, much less alarmed.

"Oh, I see," he said. "I can see you are really angry about that. Why don't you tell me about what happened?"

I have no idea why, but I spilled my guts to this guy. I told him everything—about going to church as a kid, about giving testimonies, about Flash beating me, about running away from home, about joining the Diciples . . . all the way up to my conviction and time in prison and getting LaFonda's letter days before my parole.

"I can see how much that hurt you," he said, "but you can forgive him for that; think of all that God has forgiven you for."

"I know," I said through clenched teeth. My fists were tightly gripped, and I brought them down hard on my legs. "I *know*—but you don't understand; I *can't* forgive him for *that*. He was my best friend! How could he stab me in the back like that?"

I was drunk, remember, and when sad people or mad people are drunk, they just get sadder and madder. So, in that state, I poured out my heart to this man like he was a priest hearing my confessional. He listened with so much compassion and genuine concern. I never felt safer or more loved. He told me that God had a plan for my life—big plans for my life—and that God loved me with a love that could not fail. We sat in silence after that, and I dozed off.

When the airplane landed on the runway, the jolt woke me up. I rubbed my eyes and remembered that my mom was waiting for me out there, and I hadn't seen her in two years either. Before the plane even stopped rolling, I had my seat belt off and almost sprinted up to the front by the door to be the first one off.

"Sir," the attendant said, "you must remain in your seat with your seat belt fastened until the aircraft has come to a complete stop."

As she said the words "complete stop," the plane put on the brakes and lunged to a full stop.

"Well, it's stopped now," I said. I crossed my arms and flexed my biceps, standing my ground. I guess it wasn't worth the effort for her, and the aisle was too full of passengers by then to send me back to my seat.

Outside, Mom and Flash were waiting. Mom was smiling.

She grabbed my face between her hands and said, "Let me look at you, son!"

Flash hugged me awkwardly around my waist and felt the gun. He grabbed the handle and said, "Duane Lee, what are you doing? What do you think you are doing?"

"Oh, son," my mom said, shaking her head no.

"Mom, I'm killing him," I said. "I am going to kill Jim Darnell. I am going to get LaFonda and the boys back."

"You can't, Duane Lee. Remember God has a plan for your life!" she said firmly.

The redheaded stranger came to my mind.

"Oh, Mom, Dad, you have to meet this guy I sat on the plane with! We were all the way in the back, so he'll be one of the last to come off."

I turned around to watch until the last passenger came through the door, followed by the flight crew.

"Hey!" I said to the attendant who had served me all the alcohol. "Did you see that guy I was sitting with get off the plane? I must have missed him. Did you see him?"

She looked confused and maybe a bit amused. "Sir, no one was sitting on the plane next to you. The window seat was empty in your row on this flight."

"No, no!" I told her. "He sat right next to me. He was tall. He was thin and really light-skinned. He had flaming red hair—you couldn't have missed seeing him. We talked the whole flight!"

She shook her head and kept on walking.

"Mom?" I looked at her. "He was there. He sat next to me . . . He said the most incredible things. He knew things about my life . . . I wanted you to meet him."

My mom turned my shoulders so we could look each other in

the face. She studied me for a minute, then said, "Son, I believe you did sit next to a redheaded man on that airplane—a redheaded angel. You were sitting next to an angel! And I am sure he told you exactly what you needed to hear."

I did not kill Jim Darnell.

The angel was right. God did have a plan for my life, and that plan did not include going back to prison for murder. Reluctantly I gave Flash my gun, which he locked up, and Grandpa Mike hid all his rifles, but I really struggled with forgiving Jim. Living in my parents' basement, I was depressed. The strict prison regimen had been good for me. Restricted access to things like drugs and alcohol and getting plenty of exercise while inside the joint had kept my mind clear. I had a job to do every day, and I focused on helping other prisoners, so I had a purpose. Inside I was respected by inmates and guards alike.

Out here, I was nobody, and I had nothing but free time on my hands. It was crazy-making. All I wanted was to numb the empty feeling, so I popped Valium to stay in a stupor. When I was lucid, I moaned about LaFonda and talked about wanting to kill Jim. My mom encouraged me to look for a job and stop stewing over LaFonda.

"You are not in love with her, son; you are in love with the memory of her," she said. "Do you love God?"

"Mom, you know I do!" I answered.

"Do you trust Him?" she prodded.

"I guess," I answered, staring at the floor.

"If you trust God, you have to trust Him with this too," she said as she patted my shoulder. "God will give you the desires of your heart—everything you desire. Look at what He has given you. He gave you His Son, Jesus. He gave you His house, His heaven. He gave you every blessing, even the angel who visited you on that airplane. But, Duane Lee, there is one thing He will not give you."

I looked at her. "What?"

"His vengeance." She paused. "God will not give you His vengeance, son."

I started crying. Bitter, angry tears. My hatred for Jim was a hard knot in the pit of my stomach.

"Will you rob God?" she asked.

"No, Mama, never!" I said, but my mind went to tithes and offerings. The "Will a man rob God?" scripture was always used just before they received an offering.[1] I didn't see where she was going with this. I didn't have any money to put in a collection plate.

But she said, "'Vengeance is mine; I will repay, saith the Lord.'[2] If you insist on finding Jim Darnell and you shoot him, you will rob God of His vengeance."

She let that sink in.

"You would not rob God of His vengeance, would you, son?" she asked.

My mom knew me so well. She knew my respect for God even when I saved none for myself. She knew that if she put it to me like that—"Duane Lee, if you point a gun at Jim Darnell, you are pointing a gun at God"—I could never go through with it.

Then she hugged me hard. She didn't care that I hadn't showered in days. She didn't care that I stank, that I hadn't combed my hair. She didn't care that I was irritable and depressed and focused solely on myself and my problems at that moment. She cared about me. *Mom cared about me*, and she wasn't about to let me waste my life crying in her basement.

But old habits die hard. I have always looked for love—longed for love. I always craved someone I could love and someone who would love me. Beatings from Flash were not the only abuse I endured in my childhood. There was sexual abuse too. A teenage babysitter had fulfilled her curiosity and fantasies on me with some regularity. Later, Flash introduced me to his magazines and modeled the kind of behavior that leaves a lasting impression on a boy's mind long after becoming a man.

In my mind, the pursuit of love got tangled up with the pursuit of sex. Love and sex got all mixed up until they were the same thing. Sex was proof of love. If I loved a woman, I showed her by having sex with her. If a woman loved me, she proved it by having sex with me. I know better now, but my twenty-something self could not distinguish the difference between the two.

So I was soon entangled with a woman named Anne Tegnell. The relationship quickly turned sexual, which ended up in a shotgun wedding. I'll give you a rundown on the women and children in my life shortly, but in these early days when I was fresh out of prison, I went back and forth between making really good, positive progress and really stupid mistakes that set me back.

Crime is not the only thing that can put a man in prison. Sin can do the same thing, only sin is a prison of your own making. I had yet to learn that the bondage from my past was baggage I would carry around with me for way too long.

The Dog was out of prison, but in some ways, the prison was still inside me.

FIVE

HUNTING
DOG

He was a mighty hunter before the Lord.

—Genesis 10:9 KJV

LIFE ON THE ROAD WITH HERMAN WAS GOOD FOR ME. IT KEPT me from hooking up with my old biker friends, and I loved the competitive aspect of sales. Whatever any other salesman did, I wanted to beat him. I liked pushing myself, and I got into a routine of rising very early in the morning, and I was still going strong all the way into the evening. I was so good at sales—it surprised even me.

Kirby often had sales competitions and offered great incentives to perform well, and I never missed my chance to win something. Trips, prizes—I even won a boat! On the trips, they had us listen to motivational speakers, and I heard Zig Ziglar speak several times. I started taking his seminars and practicing how millionaires thought and behaved.

I was introduced to the book *The Power of Positive Thinking* by Norman Vincent Peale, and I learned that success was not about any circumstances I had been dealt—success was in my mind. Zig Ziglar taught me, "You are who you are and what you are because of what has gone into your mind. You can change who you are and what you are by changing what is in your mind."

I realized I had to *think* and *speak* my way to success and spend no time worrying or complaining about things. Instead, I needed the confidence to believe in myself and expect things to go my way. And it worked. I might have dressed like a biker, but I sold like a tycoon!

I felt good. I was making good money, and I was respected and respectable. I didn't see myself as an ex-gangster, ex-criminal, ex-con, or ex-anything. I saw myself as a successful salesman—a successful man. I had a reason to get up every morning, and I welcomed each new day.

For years LaFonda had denied me any access to my boys, but once she learned I was doing well she suddenly filed for child support—and back child support from day one of entering prison. I did not begrudge my boys the financial support; I just wanted to be part of their lives, but LaFonda saw only detached dollar signs. She wanted money but not visitation.

When I appeared in court, another link in my destiny chain was made. The judge sat reviewing my record—my long, colorful record—and mentioned a note from Warden Horton praising me for helping recover an escaping convict (Bigfoot). He asked me if I was good at tracking down criminals.

This was a pretty strange question from a judge in the middle of a child-support hearing, but I told him, "I can track anything you ask me to track. I have been a hunter and tracker my whole life."

Then he asked me if I had ever heard of a bounty hunter.

A bounty hunter? I thought. *There it is again.* This was the third time someone had mentioned being a bounty hunter to me, so he had my attention.

The judge had me approach, then he showed me a mug shot and asked if I thought I could find him. He told me that if I brought him in, the court would cover some of the child support I owed.

That sounded like an excellent idea to me! I studied the photo like I had to pass an exam and thought about what I'd learned from the Zig Ziglar seminars. If I *believed* I could catch this guy, then I *knew* I would catch him. There was zero doubt in my mind.

I showed up that day expecting to be treated like a criminal or, worse in my book, a deadbeat dad, but instead, the sheriff took me to his office and gave me copies of the mug shots and the arrest warrant. I thanked him, but I didn't exactly know where to start. I just believed I could catch this guy. I knew I could use what I learned inside the joint about criminal behavior to get inside this guy's head and figure out what he was most likely to do and where he was most likely to go.

I looked up his mother's name and called her, pretending to be a DJ, and told her that her son, Gerald, had won a prize, but we couldn't reach him. I baited her with the promise of a $1,000 stereo if he showed up at the electronics store where I told her we were broadcasting live.

About thirty minutes later, in walks Gerald to claim his prize. *That worked?* I thought. *This is too easy!* But now that I had baited the hook and my bail jumper swallowed it, I wasn't sure what to do next. It never occurred to me what I would do with him once I caught him.

I didn't own handcuffs, so I used my belt to tie his wrists. I didn't even know where I was supposed to take him, so I went to the courthouse and looked inside all the courtrooms—with court in session—until I found Judge Levi, who was irritated at first when I barged in, but then he was impressed I had caught him so quickly. Afterward, the judge introduced me to a bail bondsman named Lucky, and I officially became a bounty hunter.

———

I had just gotten my first taste of "people hunting," and I was hooked. I wanted to do more of that. As a kid, my dad and Grandpa Mike taught me to hunt and track animals, and I seemed to have a natural instinct for it. I had learned how to stalk an animal without tipping it off. I could recognize tracks and disturbances in the brush as well as identify animals by their feces.

I used all my senses to hunt prey, and I got good at camouflaging myself to become virtually undetectable. The times hunting and tracking with my dad and Grandpa Mike were some of the only happy memories I had with Flash growing up, but it was nothing compared to the adrenaline rush and mental challenge of tracking humans.

I went to the local army surplus store and picked out a really big bulletproof vest that looked like it was left over from World War II. I bought a helmet that looked more suited to playing football than catching bounties! Then I outfitted myself in camouflage pants and a green army T-shirt. Being an ex-convict, I wasn't allowed to legally purchase a gun, so I bought a starter pistol that looked like a .22, but it was loaded only with caps. I brandished it like I meant business, though!

Since I wasn't officially in law enforcement, nobody issued me a badge—but I wanted a badge, so I ordered one from a comic book. I filled out the form with my name, Duane Chapman, and asked for the badge number to be 271097—my prisoner number. It was time to redeem that number! It took three weeks for the package to arrive, and I checked the mailbox every day, waiting for it to show up.

When it finally came in, my mother took my badge, anointed it with oil, and prayed a long prayer over it for my safety and supernatural ability to track down and catch criminals. I still remember some of the words of her prayer. "He will catch them because You sent them, Lord; they can run, but they can't hide!" she prayed. I carry this same badge to this day, and I gave my first book the title *You Can Run but You Can't Hide.*

I guess I have always been a bit of a rebel at heart, and I was still a little bit of a biker boy. I liked wearing leather vests with my tattooed guns on display. I always had my signature sunglasses, and I wore my hair then (and now) in a long, blonde mullet, often with feathers as an homage to my Apache heritage. I was an ex-convict and a successful salesman. I could hunt and track anything, and I was a closet counselor and preacher. In other words, I was everything a good bounty hunter needed to be.

The Bible says, "Ye shall know them by their fruits,"[1] so whenever I got a copy of a warrant, I looked up their record. My motto was, "By their rap sheet, I shall know them." I wanted to know if a guy was violent or likely to use a weapon on me before I met up with him.

Remember those early days when my mother took me with her to pray over people? Well, that gift of knowledge I had as a child was now put to use outside the walls of a church. In the same way that I could look at someone back then and just *know* they had an issue with alcohol or anger or lying, I had the same heightened senses with criminals and bail jumpers. If I could just look them in the eye, it was like I knew the deal before they ever said a word. I firmly believe that the Holy Spirit gave me this gift partly because He knew I would one day be a bounty hunter.

That might sound strange to you, but in Romans, the apostle Paul said God's gifts are irrevocable.[2] I believe God gives them to you before you are born, while you are still in your mother's womb,[3] and He doesn't take them away from you just because you sin. God's gifts aren't just meant for people who choose to work in a church or ministry—we *all* have gifts. Every one of us.

One translation says that "God's gifts and his call can never be withdrawn," and another says they "are without repentance."[4] So I know that the gifts God gave me as a child were meant for me to use in whatever vocation I chose as an adult, and let me tell you, the gift of knowledge has come in really handy as a bounty hunter!

I used my former experience as a criminal to outsmart other criminals. I knew how criminals thought. I could read body language and observe patterns in their behavior. I could follow the people they hung out with or find their favorite haunts. With a little patience, I could wait for them to slip up. I had the luxury of being able to make mistakes and learn from them. All they had to do was make *one* mistake for me to catch them.

My grandpa taught me that when you hunt animals, you use deception—products that eliminate or mask your scent so the prey is less likely to detect your approach. Using deception helps you control the path your prey takes and lets you study them and gather the information you need so you can determine how you will catch them.

When I hunt people, I also use deception. I find ways to get them to lower their guard and trust me. It is much safer to take someone in who doesn't know they are being caught than to take someone down while they are running from you. So creative storytelling is a big part of my bounty-hunting arsenal.

"Do you mean it is okay to lie?" fans ask.

I'm not advocating lying; I am saying that using resourcefulness, cunning, and creative storytelling is sometimes necessary for my line of work. You can call it whatever you want.

In Exodus, Pharaoh grew worried because his Hebrew slaves were multiplying so quickly that he feared they would revolt against him. He sent for the Hebrew midwives and commanded them when they delivered a Hebrew baby to let it live if it was a girl, but if it was a boy, they were supposed to kill it. But the midwives were more afraid of God than they were of Pharaoh, so they didn't kill any of the baby boys.

Angered, Pharaoh sent for them and questioned them about why they didn't obey him and instead saved the children. The midwives lied to Pharaoh—see that, right there in the Bible, they *lied*—and told him, "Hebrew women are not like Egyptian women; they are vigorous and give birth before the midwives arrive."

My favorite part is that *God was pleased with and dealt well with the midwives*. God praised them for their cunning and rewarded them with houses and children of their own.[5] Apparently, God likes resourcefulness and appreciates creative storytelling. So I decided it was a good thing to be cunning. If that means I use that cunning to set a trap to catch a bad guy, that seems biblical to me.

One of my early bail jumpers was a man out on bail for armed robbery. I knew from his rap sheet that he had guns and didn't mind using them, so I didn't want to get caught in a firefight with him and my starter pistol! I called him up and said, "Hello, my name is Duane Chapman, and I am a bail bondsman. Are you aware you have an arrest warrant out against you?"

"Uh, yeah," he answered.

"Listen, I can help you, but I need to meet with you in person so we can talk about collateral and discuss your options. I don't even care if you bring a gun; I am coming alone. Will you agree to meet me at the White Spot diner?"

He agreed, and I got there first. I positioned myself at a table where I could see him approach through the front door. I took in all the surroundings and made mental notes of everyone sitting in the diner, so by the time he arrived, I had a plan.

"Hey!" I greeted him. I could see he was nervous. His eyes were darting all over the place, and he was jumpy. I showed him both my hands and nodded my head for him to take a seat in the booth across from me.

As he slid in, I said, "I'm really glad you came, brother; the Feds are starting to close in on you. Do you see that lady over there to your right?" I gestured with my head.

"What about her?" he asked.

"Well, she's FBI. She's a G-lady, bro. And you see those two guys behind me near the back door?" I stayed looking straight ahead at him, but he looked over my shoulder, and his eyebrows went up in alarm. "They're Feds too," I said. "They are there in case you try to go out the back. I was already here when they came in and showed your mug shot to the cashier, so you better be glad I'm sitting here with you now; otherwise . . ." I shrugged my shoulders.

He swallowed hard. I pushed a glass of ice water toward him.

"Here's the deal," I said quietly and leaned in. "Brother, you are going to jail today. You can either go in with me, and I'll help you get right back out, or you can go with them and get lost in that cell for weeks or months before you get another bail hearing."

His nostrils flared, and he clocked the woman on his right again and glanced at the guys in the back. His mouth twitched, and I could see the panic rising.

"You got a gun on you?" I asked.

"No, man, I didn't bring a gun," he said.

"Good. That's better for you," I said. "I told all three of them that I would talk to you and keep you calm, and they could arrest you peacefully out in the parking lot. But the thing is, if I have you in custody—cuffed—they have no legal right to arrest you. They can't do one thing about it but watch me take you in."

He studied my face hard, trying to determine if I was telling the truth.

"I know what you're thinking, but I am not a Fed. Look at me; this mullet ain't no wig! I am going to pass you my handcuffs underneath the table. All right? You take them and put them on. If you stand up without cuffs, they've got you. If you have my cuffs on, then that means you are in *my* custody and safe from theirs," I bluffed.

"I don't know, man." He shook his head.

"Okay, stand up then. You are free to walk out that door and see what happens." I leaned back and shrugged.

He took a deep breath, then said, "Give me the cuffs," and put his hands under the table. I slipped him my handcuffs and heard him click them around his wrists.

"That's it," I said. "Now you can put your hands up on the table so they can see the cuffs. I will stand up first; then you stand up. I'll grab the cuffs, and we will walk out of here together. Okay?"

"Yeah." He nodded.

Of course, everyone in the diner was staring when I grabbed him—arms cuffed in front of him. I put a hand on his shoulder and led him out the front door. As we passed by the woman I had told him was a Fed, I leaned over and said, "Better luck next time, and thank you!"

She looked confused but politely said, "Uh, sure; you're welcome."

I walked him out to my truck as quickly as I could. I opened the passenger door and motioned for him to stand in front of it. "Now, before you climb in, as I'm sure you already know, they won't accept you from me at the jail unless your hands are cuffed behind you. Your hands have to be cuffed behind your back, or you could still risk someone else taking you into custody. Okay?"

None of this was true, of course, but the guy had no idea. I boxed him in with my body so he couldn't run and said, "Now, I am going to undo these cuffs *slowly*. When I do, I want you to put your arms behind your back and loop your thumbs together; you got that?"

He nodded and did exactly what I told him to do. No resistance.

"That's great," I said, "just like that. Now, I'm going to put the cuffs back on you; then you can climb up into my truck."

Just then, the woman from the table walked out of the diner and climbed into a little Volkswagen Bug. I pushed the guy into the truck and belted him in as fast as possible.

"Hey!" he shouted. "That lady's no Fed! You lied to me!"

I shut the door and went around to the driver's side.

"You lied to me, man!" he shouted again. "Who were those people?"

"I have no idea." I laughed. But I had my man!

Let me give you a little "Bail 101" class for those who don't know how bail bondsmen and bounty hunters work or how bail bondsmen get paid. When someone has been arrested for and charged with a crime, after the police process them, they stand before a judge who gets to set bail. If the defendant cannot pay the bail, they must wait in jail for however long it takes for their trial date.

A judge has the discretion to set the amount of bail. So depending on if this is a first offense or a repeat offense, how severe the crime is, whether the alleged crime was violent, if the defendant is employed, if he has close ties to the community or is a flight risk, and any other factor the judge wants to take into consideration, he sets the amount of the bail. Not many people have $10,000 or $25,000 or $50,000 cash on hand to cover their bail and be released, so they call a bail bondsman.

A bail bond agent works out an agreement with the defendant and posts their bail, guaranteeing to the court that the defendant will show up for his trial date or the bail is forfeited. An insurance company backs bail bondsmen.

So here is how it works: A person is arrested for a crime, appears before a judge, and, let's say, a bail of $25,000 is set. The defendant contacts a bail bondsman and pays 10 percent ($2,500) to them, which they will not get back. Typically, some sort of collateral is put up as a guarantee in case they jump bail. Sadly, it is not usually the criminal's collateral but a family member who puts up their house, car, or something valuable enough to guarantee the bail bondsman will not lose their money.

That 10 percent of the total bail amount is a fee paid to the bail bondsman for assuming the risk that the defendant will appear in court for their trial date. The bail bondsman writes a check to the court for $25,000, which the court holds. If the defendant appears at their trial, the check is returned to the bail bondsman, and they just made $2,500, and the defendant doesn't have to await their trial inside a cell.

However, if the defendant fails to appear, the court issues a warrant for their arrest. The bail bondsman is now on the hook. They must make sure that defendant appears in court before the court cashes that bail check, leaving the bail bondsman out the full $25,000. The defendant is still responsible for paying it back to the bail bond agent, but good luck collecting it! So often the bail bondsman has to take action to take possession of the collateral that was put up against the bail money. Sometimes the bail bondsman makes out better by seizing an asset than they would if the defendant showed up in court like they were supposed to. But other times the hassle of obtaining and liquidating the collateral isn't worth it.

There is money to be made in this business—sometimes good money—but the system is too easy to abuse. Many bail bondsmen out there are good guys making an honest living. There are many more who work the system and take advantage of as many as they can as often as possible.

As the clock ticks down closer and closer to the forfeiture date, a bail bondsman may call in someone like me—a bounty hunter —to help them find their bail jumper. The bounty hunter gets paid a percentage of the bond to bring the bail jumper in on time. A bounty hunter saves the bail bondsman from losing the bail they posted.

Most guys who jump bail are criminals in over their heads and fearing a long prison sentence. Otherwise, they would show up for their day in court.

Once I discovered what a bounty hunter was and started picking up bounties, I quickly built up a reputation for being the best bounty hunter in the business. I always caught my guy. To this day, the only bounty I didn't successfully capture was Brian

Laundrie, and that was because he killed himself before I had the chance. I've hunted some of the FBI's most dangerous criminals, including Andrew Luster, who made number one on the FBI's Top Ten Most Wanted list. I am the only civilian ever to catch a Top Ten fugitive, and I have captured over ten thousand bad guys in my career.

When I was starting out, I got to know all the bondsmen in Denver. My favorite, however, was a Latina woman named Mary Ellen. I liked that she was the only minority woman working in the bail bonds business in Denver. Lots of the other guys were crooked and played the game to their advantage, but Mary Ellen cared about the people she was helping.

We developed a special rapport, and she taught me a great deal about the bail bonds business. I would get to her office first thing in the morning so I could have my pick of the bounties. She was one of the hardest-working women I'd ever met. She had a good heart, but she could be tough and mean when she needed to be. After all, her business was dealing with criminals. Some of them were just guys down on their luck, but some of them were real dirtbags.

Early in my career, I began giving the guys I captured the "backseat treatment" I would one day become famous for. I wanted them to know that they could trust me to treat them right. I wasn't a cop; I wasn't a snitch. Yeah, I was ruthless on the hunt, and I would swear and cuss at them if they ran, but once I caught them, the first thing I would do was offer them a cigarette and tell them about Jesus.

It may sound bizarre to be shouting profanities at a perp one minute and then praying with them in the back seat the next— what can I say? I'm still a work in progress. Besides, shouting,

"In the name of Jesus, put your hands in the air!" didn't seem like it would be all that effective.

I had seen the hope that Jesus gave the Huntsville inmates when I was there. I wanted to share that same hope with these guys running from the law, scared their lives were over. They were not used to cops treating them with dignity, respect, or anything resembling humanity. Having been in prison and seeing how the guards treated the inmates, I had a different perspective. I always gave them a chance to come clean if they had anything hidden on their bodies before I put them in the back of my SUV. Most of them would have drugs on them and cry, "Dog, if the cops find this, they'll give me a higher bail" or "Dog, they'll give me more jail time if they find me with this."

So I would take the drugs and pour water on the powder to destroy them. If they had a crack pipe on them, I'd smash it; later on, I insisted that they smash it, wanting to encourage them to assume responsibility for their chance to change. When I did these things, they would cry even harder, "Oh, thank you, Dog, thank you!" If I was after them, they were already in enough trouble. Showing them a moment of mercy seemed like such a small gesture. A glimpse of grace.

"You're welcome, brother," I would say, then I would talk to them about getting their life right and say a prayer with them on the ride in.

I have often thought criminals are easier to figure out than women.

SIX

DADDY
DOG

*Above all, love each other deeply, because love covers
over a multitude of sins.*

—1 Peter 4:8 NIV

FANS ARE ALWAYS CURIOUS ABOUT HOW MANY TIMES I HAVE been married, and I suppose the number of marriages I have had is a little unusual. I was married and divorced four times before Beth, whom I lost to cancer. I told you earlier that I relate to King David in the Bible, and he had eight wives in his lifetime. I am now married to my wonderful Francie—a gift from God that I am grateful for every day. I think I'll stop at six.

I long for love. I hate being alone. I always have. It's no secret I had a weakness for women. After losing LaFonda and getting out of prison, I played around with the wrong kind of women until I met Anne, who I thought was a good girl, the kind of girl I wanted. I didn't know she was only seventeen, and I was forced to marry her for fear of going back to jail for violating my parole and having sex with a minor! It turns out that seventeen was legal at that time in Colorado, but by the time I knew that, we were already married, so we tried to make it work.

I did not have custody of Duane Lee or Leland when Anne gave birth to our son Zebadiah. Holding him stirred my paternal instincts, and I bonded with him instantly. But he was born prematurely and, after fighting for his life, Zebadiah went to the arms of the Lord just thirty days after he was born.

Anne and I turned to each other in our grief over our lost boy, and ten months later, Wesley was born. But things were different between us after that. We didn't fight; we just weren't connected anymore. Anne was so young when we got married, then she lost a son and had another right away. Our relationship was on-again, off-again—until she conceived . . . again.

We divorced before James Robert (J. R.) was born. I kept custody of Wesley, and she took J. R. with her back to her parents after the divorce. It really bothered me that I didn't get to see Duane Lee Jr. and Leland, and I didn't want that to happen again, but J. R. was a tiny baby, and he needed his mother. I was satisfied because at least I had Wesley with me.

Then Anne sued for custody of Wesley, and I lost the court battle. Even though I won visitation rights, Anne ignored the court's decision and moved with the boys to Utah, and I never saw her again. Both boys eventually reached out to me, but we never really had the chance to get close.

I loved all my boys, and I wanted them all with me. Leland had been just an infant and Duane Lee was a toddler when I went to prison, and they had lived with LaFonda and Jim ever since, so I barely knew them. But I wanted to change that. I went to Colorado Springs and parked outside LaFonda's house one afternoon, planning to see the boys. I even got up the courage to knock but fled before they could answer the door. The thought they might reject me made me panic, and I ran.

Alone and in pain, I did what I always do—I went looking for someone to love. I went looking for someone to love me back.

I met Lyssa sitting alone in a bar. She told me she was divorced and that her ex-husband had been a minister with the Assemblies of God, but she left him because he had been unfaithful. We started a conversation, and I learned that she had gone to Rhema Bible Training College. The fact that she loved God and understood my Assemblies of God childhood got my attention. And she was beautiful—I always fell for the pretty ones!

We got married in 1982—several months after Anne and I divorced. Soon after we were married, Barbara Katie was born, and fifteen months after that, along came Tucker Dee. He came so fast that we had no time to get to the hospital. Lyssa's water broke, but before I could even go outside to get the car, Tucker's head was crowning. I had a flashback of watching *Gunsmoke* and remembered seeing Miss Kitty deliver a baby on the show. I tried to remember what she did, but boiling water seemed stupid. I called my mom since she was a nurse. Lyssa was already pushing.

My mom said, "Reach under the baby's head, Duane, get on top. Twist the head as it comes out . . ."

"Lyssa, push. Pusssssh!" I shouted.

Whomp! Tucker came right out, but he was blue, and he didn't cry. I had never been in the room with a baby being born; they had always made me stay in the waiting room, so I had no idea what to do. I thought Tucker was dead, and I sat him on the bed beside Lyssa, who was still pushing and screaming.

Is there another one? I wondered. I saw the umbilical cord still dangling between Lyssa's legs and started tugging on it. *Woosh!* The placenta came out. Only I didn't know what a placenta was. I thought it was another baby—only that something must be terribly wrong with it!

Thank God, an ambulance driver came in right at that moment and said, "Good job, Dad, good job!" Then he cut the cord, suctioned out Tucker's nose and mouth, and started rubbing him until he cried. That cry was the most beautiful thing I had ever heard!

I kept on fighting to see Duane Lee and Leland, and after five long years, I was finally allowed to visit them on the weekends. At first they were afraid of me; no wonder—I was a stranger to them. But over time, they began to trust me, and I was determined I would be nothing like my father had been, so I showed the kids a lot of affection—hugs and kisses and playing with them. Eventually, the boys came to live with Lyssa and me.

A few years later, Baby Lyssa was born—Lyssa Rae Chapman, who soon had me wrapped around her little finger. Grandpa Mike had left his house to me. It had four small bedrooms and one bathroom, so it was pretty snug. I had so many good memories with my grandpa in that little house, and I liked raising my family there.

The neighborhood had once been nice, but it had gone downhill and was now a pretty rough place. There was lots of gang activity, and I now had six children to take care of: Duane Lee, Leland, Jason (Lyssa's son), Barbara Katie, Tucker, and Baby Lyssa. The house was too small to keep the kids inside all the time. They needed to be able to play outside, and I wanted to make sure they were safe. One night while I played with the kids out in the front yard, a bunch of gangbangers walked in front of the house. All the kids got close to me because these guys looked mean.

"That's enough!" I said, and I went into the house and got a can of spray paint. All we had was green; I don't even remember why we had it, but I grabbed it and came back outside. I followed those boys up the street about four or five houses past ours.

"Hey! You see this?" I called to them, and I painted a thick green line on the sidewalk. They all stood there, staring at me as I turned around and walked the other way past my house and down a few houses, where I painted another thick green line. I walked back to my house and painted "No Colors!" in big letters on the sidewalk.

"In between these green lines is a gang-free zone. You got me?" I said. "I don't want to see any gangbangers in front of my house or anywhere near my kids, or you will answer to me—Dog Chapman, ex-con. If you mess with my kids, I will shoot you!"

After that, we had no more trouble. They respected the green line.

We had a house full of kids to care for and bills to pay, and Lyssa and I drifted apart. I have a big personality, and I like the limelight. Lyssa was the opposite, and when Baby Lyssa was four, we went our separate ways. When we divorced, Lyssa took her son, Jason, but I kept the rest of the kids with me. At one point, I also had my nieces, Bridgette and Jennifer, staying with me. I was a single dad—Daddy Dog. Dogs are pack animals. I am too.

I threw myself into fatherhood. I learned how to make spaghetti and meatloaf and Hamburger Helper. At night, we took turns saying the blessing over our meal, and Baby Lyssa always prayed, "God, please give us a mother." I shopped for groceries and did laundry—there was no such thing as permanent-press clothes, so I ironed their clothes for school every day. I ironed everything until I taught Leland; he took over when he was about twelve. I am still an expert at ironing—a skill Francie is very pleased I have!

I kept selling Kirby vacuum cleaners and hunted bounties to make ends meet. There were always seven or eight kids plus me, so a trip to a restaurant was never less than a hundred bucks! We always had to ask the waiter for an extra bottle of ketchup because they would empty the bottle before it made it all the way around the table. We still said grace, even in public, and whenever we ate out, someone would come up to us and say, "Wow—those kids are so well-behaved. How do you get them to behave like that?"

"I threaten to kill them," I would always growl, and everyone at the table would laugh.

There were school supplies times eight, school clothes times eight, and the girls could get me to buy them stuff just by smiling and saying, "Pretty please, Daddy!"

I took the kids to church on Sundays and tried to teach them about my faith in God. I wanted to be a good man and a good role model. On Saturdays, I took the kids hunting or fishing. My girls were great at tracking. And I taught them all that Grandpa Mike had taught me—how to recognize scat and tell how fresh it was and know which poop and what tracks belonged to what animal. All the kids could track, all the kids could hunt, and all the kids could bounty hunt too. I loved being a dad. I still do.

But I wanted my kids to have a mother. When I first met Tawny, she was broken. I arrested her on a possession-of-narcotics warrant. A few years later, she showed up at my company, AAA Investigations, with bookkeeping experience and asked for (maybe demanded) a job. I am a sucker for turnaround stories—I am one—so I hired her.

I was still taking care of all the kids on my own, and I was lonely for a woman's company. Tawny was pretty, and I soon fell into old ways that resulted in Tawny moving into a guest room. The kids liked her and started calling her mom. She even went to church with me and raised her hands and either tried or pretended (I'm not sure which) to be what I was looking for. I felt like she tricked me into marrying her, even though I knew it was a big mistake.

I honestly thought I could fix Tawny. I knew she had been an addict, but I thought she was clean at the time we got married. At first, she was good at hiding it, and she settled into the family and tried to become a wife and mother. That didn't last long, though; she was back on drugs within a few months.

I don't think she was at all ready for the demands of taking care of so many children, and it clearly overwhelmed her. "Mom, what are we having for dinner?" "Mom, can you find my shoes?" "Mom, I need thirty cupcakes for school tomorrow!" "Mom, can you help me with my homework?"

It was too much for her, and Tawny would sometimes disappear for days on end. Sometimes more than a week went by before she surfaced again, so I knew she had gone back to using. She used our food money for drugs. She used the money for the electric bill for drugs. Later in life, I am sad to say, I suspect she got Tucker hooked on drugs. Again and again, she convinced me she wanted to kick the habit, and we would get her clean for thirty days or sixty days, but then something would set her off, and she was right back on the stuff. Tawny was never going to change.

We separated in 1993, not long after I moved to Hawaii and sent for her and my kids. Tawny and I had no children together. We didn't get a divorce, though. Staying married but separated was my protection against getting married again! I was back to being a single dad once more.

I didn't have the luxury of a babysitter, so sometimes I had to take the kids with me on bounty hunts. I would give Tucker or Baby Lyssa a photo of our bail jumper and make them study it—"You see that mole on his chin?" or "Notice that scar under his right eye?"—and I pointed out all the distinguishing marks until they had them memorized so they could be sure it was him even if he had on a hat or was wearing glasses or something. And then I would give them a picture of a puppy or a kitten and have them go knock on the door. "Mister, have you seen my lost puppy? He ran away, and I am trying to find him."

Disarmed because it was a child knocking, he would open up and say, "Oh no, I'm sorry, I haven't seen your dog." After he closed the door, my kid would come back to the car and say, "It was him, Daddy! He had a scar just like the picture," and I knew I had my man!

As a bounty hunter, I can knock on doors and enter houses without a warrant. So once I was sure my fugitive was inside, I would send the older kids around to all the corners of the house with flashlights, instructing them to walk very quietly and not to turn them on until I gave them the signal.

Boom! Boom! Boom! I would knock on the door.

"Come out with your hands up!" I would shout. "We've got the place surrounded!"

Then the kids would flip on all the flashlights. It was impressive.

"The sheriff and all his deputies are out here," I would bluff until the guy surrendered. Once I had him in cuffs, I would say, "You can come out now, Sheriff, thanks for your help!" and the kids would come running back to the truck to a very confused bail jumper who had just been surrounded by children!

———

Tawny and I were separated for years. I had moved to Honolulu and knew she was still somewhere on Kona, but we had no contact, and I didn't know where she was anymore. In 2002 I filed for divorce from Tawny, but I didn't know where to serve the papers. I went to the judge to file the paperwork for a "Notice by Posting." He looked at me and said, "You mean to tell me that Dog the Bounty Hunter can't find his wife?"

"Your Honor, I put an ad in the newspaper to look for her, but I didn't get a response."

He shook his head. "No, I am not going to grant this. I am giving you an extension of six months on these papers. That should give you ample opportunity to bring her in."

So I went back to Kona to find Tawny and get her to sign the papers. That was the end of marriage number four.

Beth is the wife that all the fans knew. I first met her in 1988, but we didn't get together until a few years later (while I was still married to Tawny), and we didn't get married until 2006—four years after I divorced Tawny. Together Beth and I did *Dog the Bounty Hunter*, *Dog and Beth: On the Hunt*, and *Dog's Most Wanted*. I was attracted to Beth. She was pretty, intelligent, and tough as nails. I prefer a strong, independent woman. She was a bail bondsman, and I was a bounty hunter, so getting together made sense.

Beth already had Cecily before we were married; together we had Bonnie Joanne and a few years later Garry. In 1991, I discovered I had another son I never knew about from a teenage relationship with Debbie White. His name is Christopher Michael Hecht. Neither Christopher nor I knew about each other until after the tragic suicide of his mother.

The rundown of my children looks like this:

- Christopher Michael Hecht—from a teenage romance—his mother was Debbie White
- Duane Lee Chapman (1/21/73) and Leland Blane Chapman (12/14/76)—sons from my first wife, LaFonda
- Zebadiah Chapman (1/1/80–1/31/80), Wesley Chapman (11/14/80), and James Robert Chapman (3/2/82)—sons from my second wife, Anne
- Barbara Katie Chapman (6/8/82–5/19/06), Tucker Dee Chapman (9/8/83), and Lyssa Rae Chapman (6/10/87)—children from my third wife, Lyssa
- Cecily Barmore-Chapman (6/19/93, daughter of Beth and Keith), Bonnie Joanne Chapman (12/16/98), and Garry Chapman (1/28/01)—my children with Beth

That makes twelve in all—and I have since learned that there is *one more*, but I'll save that for another chapter!

Every child is a gift from God, and I view each of my children in this way. We had a very unconventional, nontraditional family. Most children live with their mothers following a divorce, or there is some sort of joint-custody situation. Most of my children have lived with me, and I have been there for them. I made many mistakes along the way, but I have always loved them and done my best to provide for them and raise them to know that I loved God.

I was an ex-con. I made a living from my involvement as a

bail bondsman and bounty hunter in a world that most families do their best to stay far away from. There was rough language in the house. The kids saw rough characters up close and personal. I had seasons of depression followed by substance abuse. They had the instability and uncertainty of revolving mother figures and girl-friends and nannies. But they always had me—I was a constant they could count on, no matter what!

The spotlight was on them after *Dog the Bounty Hunter* took off and we had cameras and crew with us. Reality TV and reality-reality are not necessarily the same thing. The show was a real-life drama, but it was drama, make no mistake. And having a film crew with you all the time and living as a celebrity is not the easiest environment for people to develop their character or work out their issues. It took its toll. Not everything was perfect in our family, but we did the best we knew how.

Today I have strained relationships with most of my adult chil-dren, and there are different reasons for the strain with each one of them. But no matter what, I love them, and I am proud that they are Chapmans. I am proud to be their father.

The abusive discipline my father unleashed on me left an emotional scar. I vowed I would never use harsh discipline on my children, and my fear of their rejection kept me from being firm at times when I needed to be. I was so afraid of losing their love that I often toned down correction. In the same way that child-hood abuse twisted the meaning of sex and love for me, childhood abuse also confused the meaning of discipline and correction. I couldn't tell the two apart very well.

So I went light on both. I was sometimes too permissive and let whichever woman was in the picture be the disciplinarian. I always wanted to be the good guy. Of course, it is much easier to look back and think about what you might have done differently, but I was the best father I knew how to be. I loved—and still love—my children with my whole heart.

I regret that the kids saw me chasing after women, though I am not sorry any one of the kids was born. I am sorry that when I drank alcohol, my morality went out the window. I made terrible decisions when I was drunk, and sometimes there were consequences for those choices that happened while I was also a father taking care of his children. I make no claims that I was a perfect dad, only that I was a loving one.

I am proud that my kids never had a reason to lie in bed like I did and pray, *God, don't let him beat me again*. I am proud that they were never embarrassed to take their clothes off in a locker room because of bruises covering them from being beaten. I am proud that the kids know that alcohol compromises good judgment, and for the most part, they stay far away from it. I am proud I never "tied one on" with the boys or took them out drinking.

While writing this book, someone asked me, "If you knew you were about to die, and you had only a few minutes to leave a note behind for your children to read, what would you want them to know? Even if you were not able to make things right between you, what words would you want your kids to have from you?"

That question hit me hard. I wasn't sure what to say at first. I just sat there, speechless. I have a lifetime—each of their lifetimes—of history with them. Sitting there, my mind flashed back to memories of their childhoods. Things we did together, fun we had, special moments, and difficult ones too. I thought about some of the more recent disagreements, and I couldn't help but cry.

My emotions came up because of how much I care about my children. I know my kids are all adults now. They are no longer children, and some hurts and misunderstandings are hard to get past. Some actions are difficult to patch up. I have pain, and they have pain. But we all have a bond—an unbreakable bond called *family*. We are Chapmans.

So many things have been said between us, and too many things have gone unsaid. With some of my children, the history is hard, and the present looks pretty scorched between us. Some I have little or no contact with. I would give a lot for the opportunity to be reconciled with each of them. I know that forgiveness does not mean you minimize or forget things that happened between you. Forgiveness does not always mean reconciliation.

You may not have the luxury of telling your side of the story, and you may not get to have a restored relationship. Maybe one party doesn't want to engage or isn't even willing to talk. Walking in forgiveness with unresolved business out there may be the hardest thing I have ever been challenged to do. I would much rather chase down a dangerous bad guy where I might get shot than chase down emotions and memories where I might get rejected. But I know that forgiveness is a choice—a very hard choice. Forgiveness is a way to obey God, and I want to do that. I'm trying to do that.

When the woman asked me what I wanted my children to know, I looked at her and said, "I don't know too many fathers in this world who love their children as much as I love mine." And I meant it.

My mother and Grandma Annie raised me to believe in God and that the supernatural power of God is still alive and at work today. I have never strayed from this belief, even though many of my choices and actions have not always stacked up with my Christian faith. Sometimes the way I behaved was the opposite of what the Bible teaches, but I tried to raise all my kids to believe in the supernatural power of God. I want them all to know that God loves them and created each one of them with a purpose.

I wandered around for years. I would repent and step into the light, then slide back into the lusts of the flesh before repenting again—always believing in and loving God but allowing my old nature to have free rein. I am still a work in progress and am just beginning to step into the light fully. I am surrounding myself with people who will hold me accountable to grow deeper and deeper in my walk with the Lord. I have always felt close to God, but I am closer to Him now than ever before in my life, and I want my children to know His power and favor like I do.

They may wander, they may roam, they may stray just like I did, but I believe the Scripture when it says, "Train up a child in the way he should go: and when he is old, he will not depart from it."[1] I am living proof that verse is true. My mother had grace for me when I was out doing things I shouldn't have been doing. She prayed for me every day of her life. God had grace for me when I took the scenic route to His mercy instead of walking the straight-and-narrow path. So I have grace for my children to walk whatever path they choose to follow, and I trust that the same God who chased after me will chase after them and make Himself known. I trust that my kids will not depart.

———————

Whatever impacts parents impacts their children. When I sold Kirby vacuums, I was exposed to Zig Ziglar seminars, I read books like *The Power of Positive Thinking,* and later I got connected to the amazing Tony Robbins. These things were huge influences in helping me turn my life around and see a different future. You won't believe how events like these set me up for my future. Only God could have orchestrated them; I can't wait to tell you more about it.

SEVEN

TOP
DOG

But God is the Judge:
He puts down one,
And exalts another.

—Psalm 75:7

MY DAD WAS A HEAVYWEIGHT CHAMPION WHILE IN THE NAVY. Flash had to be number one at everything; he would not settle for being number two. His kids got blue ribbons because no other color ribbon mattered. You were number one or you were a loser. So even as a kid, all I ever wanted was to be number one. Long before I got my nickname Dog, I had to be the top dog—in everything.

When I was released from prison, I knew God had given me a second chance. My mother told me again and again, "So shall My word be that goes forth from My mouth; it shall not return to Me void, but it shall accomplish what I please, and it shall prosper in the thing for which I sent it."[1] She would remind me of the words spoken over me that I would serve God and preach the gospel— that I had been sent—so I don't think it was possible for me to escape from God's call.

My mom put so much of God's Word into me that it always came to the surface. I even quoted Scripture when I was running with the Diciples and when I was stone-cold drunk. Scripture verses just popped into my head for every occasion, and I credit my mom and my grandma for making sure that foundation was solid. If the Word of God is in you, it won't return void.[2] There was nowhere I could run from God.

I also had sense enough to learn from the people God put in my path. Grandpa Mike never worked for anyone; he was always his own boss. He always had a business and told me, "Duane Lee, you won't ever be successful working for someone else."

He was right. I dropped out of school in the seventh grade, so there were not a lot of exciting job opportunities out there for me. When I first decided to leave the gang life, I tried working for a beef-packing plant. They put the cattle into this long chute on their way to be slaughtered. The closer they got to the killing spot, the more terrified the cows became. Their mooing turned to screams, even though they couldn't see what was about to happen.

"Why do they scream like that?" I asked a coworker.

"Because they know," he said. "They smell the blood."

I lasted about three hours before I quit. I couldn't handle animals being slaughtered.

Then I tried a job as a tree trimmer. That worked fine while I was on the ground loading limbs into the back of a truck, but when they put me up in the bucket—no good. The boss raised it high into the air, then shook the bucket, some kind of hazing or something. I already didn't like heights, and that did me in. I shouted for him to put the bucket down, but he just took it higher and shook it again.

That was my last day on the job.

After that, I went to work on an oil rig. At lunch, you were supposed to ride down what they called a Geronimo line to get to the bottom of the derrick. But I couldn't do it. I had to walk down all those steps to get to the bottom. By the time I made it, it was time to climb them again to go back to work. On top of that, every guy I worked with was missing a finger or a hand or had a massive scar somewhere, and it was filthy work.

It wasn't for me. I quit that job too.

I saw an ad in the newspaper that offered "$200/week, guaranteed! Come let us show you what we are selling!" That's how I met Dale Newman Hunt. Selling Kirby vacuums appealed to me because it was on the ground!

I went through Kirby School and then out on the road, where I demonstrated vacuums every day but didn't sell a single one. After three weeks, Dale told me they were going to let me go. "But you said $200 guaranteed. You said all I had to do was knock on doors and show vacuum cleaners."

"Yeah, in the beginning, son, but I can't keep paying you $200 a week to sell nothing!"

I begged him for another chance. "Give me one more week," I said. "Let me go on the road with you guys, and I promise I will sell."

Dale agreed, and on the next call, he watched what I did. I had given a great demonstration, but it yielded no sale. Dale took over and closed the deal. "We have to teach you how to close," he said. And that's what he did. First, Kirby vacuums had a 33.5-foot-long cord. When a woman would ask, "Will it reach from my kitchen all the way to my front room?" Dale taught me to say, "I don't know, ma'am, let's try it. If it does, will you buy it?"

Then you had her! Find out what will make them say yes, then go get that yes.

He taught me the handshake close and the silent close. The silent close was the most powerful—and the hardest for me because I love to talk. The Kirby was $250 from the company. Anything above $250, I got to keep. If I sold one for $350, I made a hundred bucks. When someone was on the fence, I would sweeten the deal by asking them if they had an old vacuum cleaner that they would like to trade in. When they brought it out, I would say, "Okay, this brand-new, state-of-the-art Kirby sells for $400. If I give you $50 for this old Hoover, that takes it down to just $350. Do you want it at that price?"

Then the hard part. Say absolutely nothing. If it was three awkward minutes of silence, Dale taught me not to say a word. "Even if you have to hold your lips together or look at the floor, do not speak," Dale told me. Silence after the question is powerful. The first one where I didn't blow it by talking, the lady finally said, "No, honey, I don't want to buy one." I was about to thank her for her time when she said, "But if you will give it to me at that price, I will buy two. I would like one to give to my daughter as a gift."

I never spoke during a silent close again!

After that, I got to go on the road with Bobby Z. Walker and Roy Roby, two of the top producers in the state of Texas. I saw Roy load six vacuums into the back of his car. You had to sign them out, and if anything happened to them, you were on the hook to buy them. But when I saw that Roy took six, I told Dale, "Put seven in my car!" And I sold all seven that week. When we got back, Dale told me, "Dog, it wasn't on number six that you became a winner. All you did there was meet your goal. It was when you sold number seven that you became a champion."

I learned that if I hung out with smart, successful people, I became smart and successful.

The book of Proverbs says, "Hang out with fools and watch your life fall to pieces,"[3] which is how I landed in jail in the first place.

———

When I got out of prison, Mom, probably remembering my earlier success in sales, invited a man named Herman Cadillo to the house to talk with me about going on the road with him to sell Kirby vacuum cleaners.

I was unreceptive.

He was persistent.

In the end, he showed up at my mom's house and hauled me out to his car, whether I agreed to go with him or not! He was the kind of salesman unaccustomed to taking no for an answer, and being out on the road felt good. Herman hadn't bothered to let me pack, so I didn't have any Valium with me, and he never let me have any alcohol, so in a few days, my mind was clear and bright again.

I knew no one would hire an ex-convict with a murder conviction, so I never subjected myself to the rejection of trying to get a job after I got out. Selling Kirby vacuums, no one had to know I was an ex-con—even if I still looked like a biker! Selling on the road gave me the freedom to be myself, and I liked that. A lot. Herman taught me everything he knew, and my gift of gab, my ability to read people, and my gift of making people feel better about themselves helped me sell a lot of vacuum cleaners. I was soon one of the top-selling representatives for Kirby.

The company offered a lot of motivational sales training. Listening to guys like Zig Ziglar and Norman Vincent Peale (and others) reinforced what I had learned as a child: "Death and life are in the power of the tongue."[4]

What you hear or see does not matter more than what you say. What you say is what you believe, and what you believe is what you will become. I realized that all the most successful salesmen used positive confession. That was right up my alley. I wouldn't take no for an answer in sales or in anything else in life. I still won't. If I want it, I am going to speak it, and I'm going to get it!

I already told you how I added bounty hunting to my entrepreneurial pursuit, and after doing that for a while, I opened my own company called AAA Investigations. Before long, I was making money from women hiring me to follow their husbands around to see if they were cheating. That was easy money for me, but when I would show them the evidence, and they broke down, my weakness for women and their vulnerability was a bad mix.

My mother soon put an end to that. She didn't like me getting involved in illicit relationships and said, "From now on, you are *just* bounty hunting. I will pray God gives you enough bounties."

That was that—bounty hunting was all I did, no more private investigations.

God led me to another divine appointment to help me become Top Dog. I met FBI agent Keith Paul. He taught me what he learned from the Bureau, which was invaluable law enforcement education for me. He showed me criminal warrants—never once asking for my assistance or giving me instructions—but I kept an eye out while hunting bounties, and sometimes I was able to lend my assistance.

I viewed catching bad guys as part of my calling and a way to repay my gratitude because I had been given a second chance. Keith was by far my favorite G-man. Iron sharpens iron.[5] His agent insight made me a better bounty hunter. My bounty-hunting instincts made him a better FBI agent. Fidelity. Bravery. Integrity. Keith had them all.

I have always loved connecting people. As a boy, I liked playing Cupid with my friends. From this, I learned that introducing friends to each other got me places. The boy would do something cool for me because I introduced him to a girl, and the girl would do something nice for me because I introduced her to the boy. I realized I had a gift. To this day, networking is one of my greatest assets. I have so many amazing connections in my phone—people I can call on and people I can count on—and they can count on me! If I know someone who has something that could benefit somebody else I know, I always introduce them to each other.

Keith Paul did this for me too. He introduced me to Tony Robbins. Tony is another divine appointment that helped me get to the top of my game. I tell the incredible story of how we met and how I ended up being a guest speaker at some of his events in *You Can Run but You Can't Hide.* I'll never forget when he introduced me as a great example of a "criminal gone wrong." He loved that I had taken my experiences of what I learned in jail and used it to pursue justice. There is no way to explain how we connected other than that God orchestrated it.

The crowd responded enthusiastically every time I spoke—another confirmation of those early words spoken over my life. I am a preacher at heart.

Tony invited me to speak at more of his events, and our friendship grew. I looked forward to them; they were a vacation for me where I could recharge. I always left motivated, feeling on top of the world and ready to do anything. Then Tony asked me to go through his Business Mastery seminar.

"Yeah, cool," I responded. "Do you want me to speak at it?"

"Nope," he said.

"You want me to be your bodyguard?" I asked.

"Nope," he said again. "You are going to take the course."

I wasn't sure how I felt about that. I remembered how, at one of his events, they took the lights down really low, and Tony asked people to put themselves into the worst situation they had ever endured. He would call things out like, "when you got fired," and you would hear people sigh or see them put their head in their hands, or "when someone you loved died," and you would hear people start to weep.

Tony would take them down to their lowest moment, and I wanted to bolt. I like happy things. But then, Tony built them back up from the bottom, teaching them, "All you need is within you now." It was incredible how he took them to the highest moment in their life and somehow managed to help restore their power. He has a gift.

It still didn't seem like something I wanted to go through for days, though. *I am good*, I thought. *I am a positive thinker. I speak positive words. I am a successful bounty hunter.* I didn't think I needed Tony's seminar, but he insisted. I agreed because I was grateful to him for allowing me to speak so many times. Tony teaches people how to unleash the power within, and one exercise is putting aside physical discomfort to pursue mental excellence—his famous fire walk.

Tony had me stand at the end of the line where people walked over the hot coals. He said, "Dog, I've watched you. When you see someone have a breakthrough, I see what happens to your body. I see what happens to your attitude, to your state of mind. You are a breakthrough guy!"

He had me stand there as hundreds of people did this exercise. It's incredible. People face and conquer their fears and come off those coals screaming in victory and hugging you. Tony was right; seeing people have a breakthrough is a serious high. I feel the same way when I see someone walk down an aisle at a church to respond to an altar call, or when a guy handcuffed in the back seat of my SUV decides it's time to change his life. I was born to participate in breakthroughs.

I started using what I learned from Tony on bounty hunts too. When I was scared to death that someone had a gun, I would stand in front of the door and say, "In the name of Jesus, all I need is within me now!" *Boom!* I would kick the door down and go in after my guy!

One time in Hawaii, after one of Tony's ten-day events, as people were going around the circle and sharing their plans since going through the program, I said, "This is it. I'm not leaving. This is paradise. I love it here, and all I need is within me now. I am staying in Hawaii!"

Tony had paid me $5,000 for speaking at his seminar and counseled me to add being a bail bond agent to my bounty-hunting business. Why divide the money? I decided to get a bail bonds license and set up shop in Hawaii. That $5,000 didn't last very long. Lodging, food, fees, and getting the license was harder and took longer than I expected. I got down to my last $300. I slept in my rental car parked under a bridge. First thing every morning, I went to the courthouse the minute it opened and handed out my business cards.

I still had an office running in Denver, and I went back and forth between Colorado and Hawaii, trying to keep that office afloat while establishing this one. I called my mom because I had asked her to pray. I was getting discouraged, so I said, "I don't know, Mom; what do you think about this? How do you feel?"

"Duane Lee, you asked me to pray, not to feel. What did God tell you to do?" she said.

The next week, I wrote a $50,000 bond and a $100,000 bond and had $15,000 cash! I had to pay some fees to the insurance agency, but I had enough to buy tickets for Tawny and the kids to join me in Hawaii.

I did get my business up and running in Hawaii, but I faced many obstacles that saw it shut down for a season. A few years after Tawny and I separated, I joined forces with Beth in Colorado, and we made Free as a Bird Bail Bonds a force to be reckoned with. We plastered the wall with the wanted posters of the guys we went after. I faced constant issues with insurance agencies, state regulations, other bail bondsmen, and many other hurdles. Still, I always held fast to my confession, and by God's grace, we cleared every obstacle.

Free as a Bird Bail Bonds was listed ninth in the phone book, and this was in the days before the internet when your listing in the Yellow Pages was the life of your business. I prayed and asked God how to get more business for my struggling company. He led me to *Webster's 1828 Dictionary*, where the very first word was "A." I had only ever thought of "a" as a letter, not as a word, but there it was. "'A' is the first letter of the alphabet in most known languages . . . Among the ancients, 'A' was a numeral denoting 500 . . . The Romans used 'A' to signify a negative or dissent in giving their votes."

I had my answer! I photocopied the page from the dictionary and went down to the county clerk's office to register the name of my new business, "A."

"Just 'A'?" the clerk asked. She looked very puzzled. "Sir, you can't register a letter as a business name. Do you mean A Bail Bonds? I don't understand."

"No, ma'am." I shook my head. "I want to register the name of my business as 'A,' just 'A,'" I said, and I pulled out my photocopy to show her that "A" was a word, not just a letter. "This is a subsidiary of my AAA Investigations Company," I explained. She was reluctant, but what could she do? No law prevented me from registering my business as "A."

Once all the paperwork was completed, and my business was legally registered, my next stop was the telephone company. I went in to see the receptionist, filled out the card, and requested the number 296-BAIL (2245). "You can't do that," the woman said, pointing to the form where it asked for the business name. "'A' isn't the name of a business; it is just a letter."

I pulled out my state-issued business license and the photo-copied page from the dictionary. "I beg to differ," I said with a smile, and I left with 296-BAIL as the phone number for my newly named bail bond business. I also took out a full-page ad that said, "If you want out of jail, call me!" And I listed translators available for Spanish, Filipino, Japanese, and several other languages. Of course, I didn't have anyone working for me who spoke any of those languages, but I didn't want to miss any bail money, so I figured I could find someone if I needed to!

When the Colorado listing came out, it read "A—Bail Bond Company." The phone company added the explanation, but I never requested it. I had the first listing underneath "Bail Bond Companies," and my full-page ad was on the right-hand page directly after the listings began. This infuriated the other bail bond agents, but they could do nothing about it. I was Top Dog in the phone book! I did the same thing when we got everything ironed out in Hawaii. They listed me as "A—Hawaii Bail Bonds" in the phone book, and the strategy paid off there as well.

Eventually, we became the world-famous Da'Kine Bail Bonds everyone knows from watching *Dog the Bounty Hunter*. All I can say is that with God, there are no coincidences. I know I heard

Him tell me to look in the dictionary. I'm just not that smart on my own! Every single time I listen to the voice of God, things tend to work out.

As a kid, my mom put me on the Denver-based *Fred 'n' Fae* tv show. I still remember how I felt when I watched myself on the show. I remember hearing someone say, "Look, Duane Lee is showing his best side," so I started looking in the mirror to figure out what my best side was. I think I expected to be on television after that. Maybe I didn't know when, but I knew it would happen. I knew it by faith!

My time with Tony Robbins exposed me to many celebrities. People like Ozzy and Sharon Osbourne told me I would be on television. Martin Sheen once told me, "Man, you need to be on television . . . and when they make the movie, I want to be the voice of God!" They may have been saying it to be polite or to make casual conversation, or they might have meant it heart and soul; it didn't matter—it meant something to me! I saw how they acted in public and thought to myself, *I have the same joyous personality they do. They're right—I could be on TV!*

I linked up with Boris Krutonog, who read about me in Tony Robbins's book *Awaken the Giant Within*. When he called, he was just another guy in a long line of guys who told me I would be famous and I should be on television. But in 2003, A&E did a reality show called *Take This Job*, and I was featured on an episode. They followed me (along with Leland, Tim, and Beth) around the office and on a bounty hunt. I did episodes for the *Secret World of Bounty Hunting* and *Anatomy of a Crime*. Each time we were featured, the ratings for whatever episode we were in were very high. The public liked us.

After the high-profile capture of Andrew Luster (one of the FBI's Top Ten criminals) in Mexico, and all the publicity surrounding our arrest by the Federales there and subsequent escape back to the United States (see the afterword for more on this), eventually I got a call from Boris saying he had heard from CBS, NBC, and the not-so-well-known network A&E.

The offers from CBS and NBC were higher, but neither of them would allow me to say, "In Jesus' name" or "in the name of Jesus" on the show. My mind immediately went to the verse, "But whosoever shall deny me before men, him I will also deny before my Father which is in heaven."[6] That was a deal-breaker for me. I am who I am. Jesus lives in me, and there was no way I would pretend He didn't.

Beth and I sat in a parking lot outside a steak house, discussing the offers. The other two were significantly more money, and Beth countered, "Big Daddy, you can still say, 'in the name of Jesus,' and they can just edit that part out. You don't have to change who you are. We are talking about a lot of money here." But I saw myself standing before Jesus, and I just could not bring myself to agree to that condition.

"A&E gave us our start with *Take This Job*. We are going with A&E," I told her.

"Okay, well, you know what's best then; I hope you are right," she said.

"I guess we'll find out," I said with a smile, and we signed with A&E.

After we signed all the contracts, they did try to pull a bit of a flip-flop on us. "Yes, yes, you can do whatever you want on the first few shows, but we'll see how it goes. We'll watch how the fans respond. If it causes issues with the ratings, then you'll just have to wrap up prayers with 'amen' instead."

I had already signed the contracts, and filming season one was underway. I just handed it to God and told Him, "I will never deny You. Ever. I will proudly say the name of Jesus and take whatever consequence comes."

When it came time to attend the show's premiere, Beth and I got all dressed up, walked the red carpet, and went in to view the first episode. We had not seen the show up to this point. They had cameramen embedded with us, following us around the office, at the house, in the car, and everywhere we went. They were with us all the time. We got used to them being there and didn't really think about how they were capturing every single thing we said or did. They filmed hours and hours of footage to get the twenty minutes that would be aired as an episode.

Beth and I had agreed not to let them film me giving fugitives medication, food, or cigarettes. We didn't want any of that on camera, as it went against the rough, macho image of a bounty hunter and might be bad for ratings. Showing compassion could have made us seem weak to those on both sides of the law—criminals or cops! Beth felt strongly that she didn't want any of that to be part of the show. And for Christians, the way we dressed and the fact that I cussed and went after our perps hard-core, then offered them a cigarette and prayed with them, opened us up for controversy and criticism. How different denominations might react to this could create a problem with that important fan base.

In our first episode of season one, our criminal, Floyd, was an escaped convict with the last name—you won't believe this—Chapman! Well, we got our man and put him in the back of the car. I drove in this first episode, but later I always sat in the back seat with our fugitives. Once we had all our tough talk out of the way, I asked the cameraman to shut the cameras off.

"Okay, it's off," he said.

I tilted the rearview mirror down so I could look Floyd in the eyes and said, "Now, what can we do to help you, Floyd? Do you want a drink of water; you want a cigarette? . . . You know, bra, I been right where you are at right now. I was a criminal; I was a sergeant at arms for a motorcycle gang. We robbed, we pillaged, we did everything . . . Let me tell you from experience, at the end of the criminal rainbow is not a bucket of gold. It's a six-by-six cell . . ."[7]

When we pulled into the jail's parking lot, I told the boys to let him out so he could stretch. He was barefoot, and his feet were all cut up, so we had Leland go get some bandages, then clean and dress his feet. I sent Beth to get him some cheeseburgers. We put a little money in his pocket before one of my guys took him inside. I told him to tell them that he had been cooperative and not to mention that he tried to run.

I never expected any of that stuff to have made the show. They had filmed so much of us figuring out where he was, and then the excitement of capturing him at his house. When we sat through the premiere, Beth and I were stunned that so much of the show was focused on "the backseat treatment." My stomach sank the moment I saw the image of me looking at Floyd in the rearview mirror. "Beth, honey, I didn't know—" I whispered.

"Well, this is going to be a pretty short career," she said. "It might last all of fifteen minutes!"

I thought all the stuff we did to take care of him would be stuff they left out—like cut to the commercial and show the more exciting stuff. I was completely stunned that they spent so little time on the takedown and so much time on us bringing him in. When it was over, Beth and I stood up. I just wanted to sneak out as fast as we could, but the place erupted into applause. *They liked it!* They *liked* the part where we treated the guy like a human, not a convict. It turns out my cameraman, Andrew Dunn, had done me a favor by keeping the cameras rolling!

The ratings took off. We became the number one show on A&E, and their president, Nancy Dubuc, told me, "I don't care if you say in the name of Buddha—you have broken all the records, and you can say whatever you want. It looks like you and Jesus got your own thing going!"

When the season two poster came out, I hated that they were still using the word "ex-con" to describe me, so I called Nancy. She said, "Dog, you have gone from ex-con to icon! You are Top Dog!"

And I was the top dog. I had been the top dog in sales at Kirby. I was the top dog as a bounty hunter and business owner, and now I was the top dog in entertainment. *Dog the Bounty Hunter* went into syndication and went on for nine seasons, followed by *Dog and Beth: On the Hunt* (on CMT) and *Dog's Most Wanted* (WGN). I had successful shows on three different networks.

Because I refused to deny Jesus, God had exalted me. I have no doubt that God brought me every person we captured. Whenever I cast my cares on Him, He proves again and again that He cares for me. But make no mistake, being the top dog puts crosshairs on your back. Every time I rose to the top in my life, there he was—my enemy, the devil, like a roaring lion on the prowl, looking for someone to devour.[8] He never missed his chance to take a bite out of me!

EIGHT

CAN'T KEEP A
GOOD DOG DOWN

*"In the world you will have tribulation; but be of good
cheer, I have overcome the world."*

—John 16:33

I JUST TOLD YOU ABOUT SOME OF THE HIGH POINTS IN MY life. Now I will share some of the times when I was brought low—really low. It is harder for me to tell these stories because I like to focus on all the good things in my life, and there are many. But, like you, I have had my share of dark days—and darker nights. I can honestly say, though, that even in my worst moments, God was there. He never left me. No matter what I did to try to drown out my pain or escape from grief, God kept His hand on me.

I hate losing people I love. Losing a family member, a friend, or even a pet is hard on me. I love big, and I love with my whole heart, so when someone I love dies, a piece of me dies with them.

I adored my mother. She was on a pedestal for me—like the closest thing to a saint you could meet in flesh and blood. She loved God with all her heart, and she demonstrated to me what unconditional love looked like. The way she loved me made it easy for me to accept God's love for me. It gives me pain now to recall how much pain I gave her. I know many of my life choices brought her disappointment and grief; still, she never stopped loving me. Even when she knew I wasn't living right, and even when she didn't approve, she never withheld her affection or acceptance from me, and she prayed for me every day of her life.

After she got sick in 1991, I brought her to Hawaii to live near me. When I picked her up from the airport, she took a deep breath. The air was filled with the fragrance of tropical flowers. She took my arm, smiled, and said, "Son, you brought me to the garden of Eden!"

My mother had emphysema and needed supplemental oxygen to breathe. She hated having that plastic tube around her face, and I wanted her to breathe again without needing the tube. I had read about what amazing oxygen producers hibiscus plants were, so I filled the guest room with thirty brightly colored, flowering plants. When she walked in, her eyes lit up, and she clapped her hands. "Oh, son, this is so amazing! I am in paradise!" she exclaimed. I would have put a thousand hibiscus in her room if they had fit! Nothing was too good for my mom. Mom was off oxygen and breathing freely within a month of coming to Hawaii.

I wanted her and Flash to move there so she could spend the rest of her life without any worries or cares. I looked for a rental house where they could live, but everything was way out of my price range. I was looking on Kona, the Big Island, with its breathtaking views, tropical vegetation, and crashing ocean, but the house I fell in love with was $2,500 a month.

At that time, it might as well have been $25,000 a month—I just did not have that kind of money. The owner saw my disappointment and asked why I wanted to rent this house so badly. When I told her it was because I wanted to take care of my mother and provide a place for her to end her days in paradise, she smiled and nodded. "Young man," she said, "did you know that Elvis Presley did the exact same thing for his mama, Gladys?"

I nodded my head and said, "I understand why Elvis did that. My mom means everything to me too. She has put up with so much from me; I just want to take care of her."

"I'll tell you what," she said. "My mortgage on this house is $850 a month. Do you think you can cover that?"

"You would do that for me?" I answered, stunned. "You would let me rent this beautiful home for my mother for just $850 a month?" Even then, that was a lot of money, but how could I refuse? This was God's hand of blessing not just for me but for my mama too. If He had opened this door, He would provide. So I signed the lease and moved my parents in.

Mom helped me with my bookkeeping, and Flash also helped with the bond business in Kona. You could get a ticket from Kona to Honolulu for around thirty dollars at that time, so I could fly back and forth from the Honolulu office to the Kona office, and sometimes Mom flew to me. On one of those trips, she and I drove all over Oahu together in my MG convertible.

We talked for hours and hours. When she told me I needed to learn more about my heritage one day, I thought she was talking about how she, my grandmother, and my great-grandmother had all been prophetic and heard God's voice. I think she wanted to tell me then about my real father but may have been concerned about what I would think of her, or maybe she worried I wouldn't take care of Flash if I knew. Whatever her reasons for not telling me, I have long since forgiven her. I am proud of my heritage—my Apache heritage from my father's blood and my godly heritage through my mother's line.

As we drove, Mom reminded me of the words spoken over me as a child and that I would one day preach the gospel. She told me I was okay on my own. I was a leader, I was strong, and God expected me to hear His voice and answer His call. "I do hear Him, Mom," I protested.

"Duane Lee," she said, "I have fought the good fight, do you understand?"

She had never used those words with me before, and it scared me. "No, Mom, you are better now. Your emphysema is so much better now. Don't even say things like that," I pleaded.

When I took her to the airport, it was the last time I saw her. I didn't know that, or I never would have let her board that plane. I will never forget how she looked back over her shoulder, said, "I love you, son," and winked at me.

News of her death hit me like nothing else I had ever experienced. Hearing the judge find me guilty—being convicted of a murder I didn't commit—did not feel this bad. I crawled into a bottle and tried to drink my pain away. I walked in a drunken stupor for at least twenty miles. I was wearing cowboy boots without socks. Blisters formed on my feet, then broke open and bled, and still I walked. Angry. Lost. Afraid. I realized God had been speaking to me through my mother, but I hadn't heard Him. I wasn't walking close enough to Him to recognize His voice— even when it came through someone I loved as much as my mother. I was so angry with myself and so lost without my mother to talk to.

I sunk lower and lower until my depression gave way to substance abuse, at first only with prescription drugs. I was barely functional, and it's honestly a miracle that I made any money at all during those dark days. Thank God my businesses were still operational, even if I wasn't. I hired nannies to help out with the kids because I knew I wasn't in the right headspace to give them what they needed. I think we might have gone through twelve nannies in one month at one point! In the fog of being high or drunk, the nannies (and the girlfriends) came and went. I constantly looked for someone to love—for someone to love me to take the pain away. I got involved with a woman who took me further and further from the right path.

I don't want to tell "glory stories" about when I was lost in sinful behavior. This was an ugly time in my life. I remind you that drinking alcohol has always compromised my judgment, and I made the worst, most immoral decisions when I was drunk. One of those led me to try crack cocaine, even though I didn't know that's what it was at the time. I sunk lower and lower and got deeper and deeper into the hole. Days and nights ran together.

Weeks and months passed, and I had no idea about what was happening in the world. I no longer wanted to hunt bounties. I didn't really want to do anything anymore. For a whole year, I was barely conscious. I lost weight and dropped below 140 pounds. I even stopped calling myself Dog—having God's name backward as my nickname seemed disrespectful. Instead, I started calling myself Kawani—Hawaiian for Duane. I was completely lost.

Only God's grace kept me from killing myself with that stuff, and His protection was certainly on my children because I was not thinking clearly at all. In fact, I almost lost them to social services. I didn't want to admit it, but I had become an addict. I had not touched drugs in more than three thousand arrests when drugs were readily available to me. But my grief and getting mixed up with the wrong women drove me into it. Not only could I lose my kids, but I could also lose my bail bond license if caught.

One night in desperation, I called Beth, who was still living in Denver. She flew out to Hawaii and cleaned house—Beth style! She booted out the girl who got me hooked on the stuff and scrubbed the place from top to bottom. She changed the sheets, did the laundry, filled the fridge with groceries, and was brutally honest with me about what a mess I was in. Beth was never one to pull any punches.

The next time she flew out, thank God she looked through my finances and checked on the businesses. The books were a mess. Employees had written bonds in my name, not reported them to the insurance company, and stolen money from me. When it all came to light, my insurer was holding all the cards. My only way out was to agree to stop doing any business in Hawaii for two full years.

Rumors were flying around, and I was ashamed. I had to give up the Kona house and move into a one-bedroom shack with the kids. With no job, and no income, in humiliation I had to apply for food stamps. One day at the grocery store, I tried to buy toilet paper with food stamps. The clerk announced loudly enough for everyone to hear, "Toilet paper is not food, sir. You are not allowed to use food stamps to buy anything but food." I counted the change in my pockets but didn't have enough, so I left in disgrace. *What kind of man am I?* I wondered. *I can't even afford to buy my children toilet paper!*

I can honestly say that my kids are what kept me going. If it hadn't been for them and my desire to care for them, I am unsure if I would still be alive today. In desperation, I reached out to my friend Tony Robbins after hearing he was doing a seminar on the Big Island. I had not spoken at any of his events in a long time, but he met with me and patiently listened to my long story. At the end of my tale, I asked him for a job on his security team. He said, "No, Dog. I wouldn't be doing you a favor by hiring you for that job." He gave me advice instead.

Tony reminded me that I had chosen my way into my predicament. I could blame others as much as I wanted to, but my choices had gotten me there, and my choices could get me out. I had not really accepted my mother's death, and I had spiraled so far down into self-pity that it was paralyzing me. I felt like I had no power left. "Dog, all you need is within you now," he said, thumping my chest. Then he advised me to go back to Denver, sit on a rock beside a stream, clear my head, get back to my roots, and figure out what I needed to do next.

When I left Tony, I went to the ocean and sat beside it for two straight days. At forty-four, I didn't feel like starting over. I wrestled with every possible thought. Maybe for the first time, I understood what the apostle Paul meant by telling us we needed to "demolish arguments" and "every proud obstacle that keeps people from knowing God." I sat there battling with guilt, anger, frustration, and grief. Slowly, I began to bring "every thought into captivity to the obedience of Christ."[1]

I realized I had just been stuck in a loop, complaining about my circumstances. And as my thoughts returned to God and His plans for me, I felt as if my mother was there, watching over me. I noticed a trail of footprints led from where I was sitting into the ocean, and I had seen no one else on the beach. I got up and studied them because they looked just like my mother's footprints.

Mom was telling me it was time to leave Hawaii. Memories of her flooded me—all the things she had taught me over the years. I thought of what I had learned from Tony Robbins, Zig Ziglar, and many others. I knew it was time to start over. It was time to leave Kawani behind. It was time for Dog to find his bark again!

This decision to return to Denver was followed by a long season of recovery and restoration, and I have to give Beth credit for standing by my side on that long, bumpy road to becoming whole again. I tell that story in full detail in *You Can Run but You Can't Hide*, so I won't tell it all again here. I will tell you that

I *used to be* a drug addict. By God's great grace, I have put all that behind me.

Walking through addiction gave me even greater compassion for those who are hooked on junk, though. It is part of why my "backseat treatment" is so authentic. I understand the level of pain and desperation involved in driving someone to that low place, and I also know the hold drugs have on a person and how hard it is to get—and stay—clean once that stuff has altered someone's mind and messed with his brain chemistry. *I am no longer a drug addict.* I will never touch that stuff again. This is a miracle—for sure, one of my nine lives.

———————

Another dark time for me began the night before my wedding to Beth when my beloved Barbara Katie was killed in a terrible car accident. Incredible guilt swept over me. Barbara Katie had gone for an extended visit with her mom, Big Lyssa, to Alaska. I sent her money while she was there as she asked for it, not knowing she had gotten involved with drugs and was now struggling with addiction. When I found out, Beth and I brought her baby, Little Travis, to live with us so Barbara could go to rehab, but she didn't stay the course.

Reporters tracked our family, and she feared the unwanted, negative public attention that would bring. She got pretty messed up. Beth was concerned that the pressure of a big family event all caught on film for television might be too much for her, so in the end, we decided not to send her a ticket to attend our big day. I still regret this, wondering if she might be alive today had she gotten on an airplane to join us.

I am not sure how I got through the wedding. I was numb. In shock. Angry. My pastor, Tim Storey, had come to officiate our wedding—and now I needed him to perform a funeral. With all the arrangements already made, food prepared, family and friends already there, and a camera crew from A&E present to capture this long-awaited and much-publicized event, we went ahead with the wedding.

Much about that day was happy, and I wanted Beth to have her dream wedding, but my heart was divided. I let out my emotions in private. I cried, screamed, I even howled until I was hoarse. In the end, I put my emotions in check. I put Barbara Katie's tragic death inside a box in my brain, locked it down, and forged ahead with the day. Underneath it all, though, I was really angry. Her death seemed needless, and I wanted to blame someone or something.

After the funeral, Beth and I cared for Barbara Katie's little boy, and I loved spending time with my grandson. I think taking care of Barbara's son helped me heal. I had never met the boy's father before, but I felt like I should call him and let him know Barbara had passed away. I asked if he wanted to see his son, and he did.

Eventually, this giant six-foot-nine man showed up in Hawaii, and Little Travis ran right to him. After a while, we asked him if he wanted to keep Little Travis for the weekend. Then another weekend. Eventually, I offered that if Big Travis would stay in Hawaii, work for me, and be more involved with the family, Little Travis could go live with him.

But more dark days were ahead.

I had captured Andrew Luster, a serial rapist who had skipped out on his million-dollar bond. I had chased down and caught

America's number one criminal in Mexico, which landed me in some legal and financial trouble you can read all about in *Where Mercy Is Shown, Mercy Is Given*.

My show, *Dog the Bounty Hunter*, was sitting at number one on A&E. My first book had reached the number one spot on the *New York Times* bestseller list. I traveled the country on a book tour where I met and talked with thousands and thousands of fans. My popularity soared. In more ways than one, I was on top of the world.

I got so on top, however, that I stopped "bothering God" with my problems. I called on Him for the big stuff. I still asked for His guidance to catch bad guys, but I felt like God was too important and too busy for me to interrupt Him with my problems. I trusted myself. I counted on my fame, and I started relying more on my wits and my instincts and less on Him. I still loved God, but I felt like I should dig myself out of troubles of my own making without having to concern Him with them. I felt like I should save God for the really big miracles.

Boy, was that a mistake!

I found myself canceled before cancel culture was cool.

Things between my son Tucker and I were strained. Tucker had served time for drug possession when he was younger. He had later spent four years in jail for armed robbery and was now out on parole. He wasn't doing well, from what I could see. There was tension between us. There was tension between his girlfriend and Beth.

One night, on a long, heated telephone call with Tucker, I used language I shouldn't have. My son recorded our conversation and sold it to the *National Enquirer*. The call was taken out of context. Only a small portion of it was transcribed and published;

even what was reported, when read in context, did not mean what it was portrayed as. But it was embarrassing. My words were twisted, and I was put into the absolute worst possible light.

There were crosshairs on my back, and every devil in hell lined up to keep the trouble stirred up. I was a professing Christian. Scandal and a hit to my reputation were exactly what Satan had been waiting for. I handed his opportunity to him on a silver platter.

It was certainly not my finest hour, and had I listened to God (or Beth, who told me to hang up), it would never have gotten so blown out of proportion. But I didn't listen. I ran my passionate mouth, and the result was that everything came crashing down.

I was devastated by my son's betrayal. It never occurred to me that Tucker could do something like that—not just betray me but betray me for money and actually seek to harm me. I didn't know how to process it. Even more of a shock, I was shattered that I was accused of racism—something so foreign to who I am and how I have conducted my entire life that I was stunned anyone could believe it. People who knew me well knew it was not true. Many of my African American friends stood up for me and stood with me, but once the news and tabloid snowball was rolling, it could not be stopped.

In response to pressure from advertisers, A&E paused production on *Dog the Bounty Hunter* and threatened to cancel the series. Our show was wildly popular and had millions of viewers each episode, but its future was now hanging by a thread resulting from this accusation.

Beth pulled every string she had access to. My publicist was doing damage control, and I was fighting for my reputation—which is much worse than fighting for your life. I called my mentor, Tony Robbins, who offered to let me go to Naples and lay low to ride it out until the controversy died down. Spin doctors advised me to say I had been drunk on the recorded call (it had worked for other celebrities) and offered many other terrible suggestions, but I said no. It felt like everywhere I turned, the situation just got worse and worse.

Finally—and I have no idea why it took me so long to do this—I called on God to be my defender. I prayed. I cursed the devil and asked God to remove this thorn from my flesh. Three days later, Larry King called for an interview to address the accusation head-on. A&E did not want me to do it. Michael Feeney, an executive, told me if I went on Larry King, I would be fired. But I had been on *Larry King Live* before, and I knew he was fair. I asked God about it and felt like I heard Him confirm His hand was on it. So I agreed to the interview.

Larry began the segment by pointing out that my vocabulary was limited because I dropped out of school in the seventh grade. There is no doubt that my time in a motorcycle gang, which led to serving time in the Huntsville Unit, and even what I did for a living—hunting down criminals—impacts the way I talk. "I know right from wrong," I answered. "I'm not that kind of guy. I knew I probably never should have used that. But I thought I was cool enough to be able to use that. But to blame it on ignorance and unlearned, that's not—no . . ."[2]

Larry went on to play the recording of the call, and it was painful to listen to. As we continued the interview, Larry had a poll going on CNN.com about whether people should forgive me; specifically, if they thought A&E should cancel my show. He opened the phone lines to callers and let people email in to ask me anything they wanted.

Tim Storey, my pastor and a Black man, also came on the show and stood by me. He nailed me for having a foul mouth—something he had cautioned me about many times before—but he stood by my character and, having known me for years, vouched that I had never demonstrated racist behavior in all that time. I answered a few more viewer calls and emails, and by the time the segment ended, more than sixty thousand people had gone to the website. Eighty-two percent of them voted that A&E should not cancel my show.[3]

I started bawling right there on national television.

That was not the last of those dark days, but that cracked open a door that let light in from the end of the tunnel. During that season, my Black brothers and sisters received me with open arms everywhere I went. Denzel Washington hugged me and whispered words of encouragement in my ear. Sidney Poitier had me sit with him at his birthday party, and many other actors showed me love and support. Mel Gibson told me about his rocky relationship with his son, who was now a producer. All of it humbled and encouraged me. Most importantly, my fans rallied. As bad as the fall had been, the love I got back strengthened me. You can't keep a good Dog down.

When I returned to A&E, viewership was up 37 percent over what it was before the scandal. Nancy Dubuc said, "Well, Dog, what do you have to say for yourself?"

I smiled and said, "Nancy, every dog has his day, but Tuesday night belongs to me and A&E!" The Dog was back.

But perhaps my darkest night of the soul came when I lost Beth.

Her illness took a toll. I am a man of faith. I believed with all my heart that God would heal her, and I prayed and asked Him to remove the cancer. After her first surgery, I was sure we had our miracle. When it returned, I knew we were in for a fight.

I talked and prayed with Pastor Tim. I talked to Tony Robbins. Tony even got me in touch with Deepak Chopra, and we talked about stem cells. I was willing to try anything—*anything*—to keep Beth alive. I didn't care what it cost. I wanted Beth to beat that cancer.

On my call with Tony, he said, "Dog, you have faced a lot of hard things in your life."

"I know," I answered.

"You have always been able to come out of it. You are strong, and you've got your faith. You will come out of this too. You know this isn't the whole story; you know there is a bigger plan, yes?"

"I know," I repeated.

"Dog?"

"Yes, Tony?"

"Dog, Beth is going to die . . ."

I froze. My hero was telling me my wife was going to die, and I needed to prepare for that. I needed to find the strength to walk beside her while that terrible disease stole her life away from her.

As Beth and I filmed episodes of *Dog's Most Wanted* together, she struggled. She felt tired and sick. She was losing her hair, and the team constantly worked to keep her in wigs or scarves. She kept her nails done to perfection and did "anything to keep me looking normal," as she said. On Mother's Day, she spoke an emotional message at the Source Church in Bradenton, Florida, where she talked about cancer being the biggest test of her faith.

In her final days, I went into survival mode. I stayed by her side—almost 24/7. I didn't work because Beth would get very upset if I left the house, afraid she might die while I was away. She thought she had months left, but it turned out to be days, and I can't even recall how numb I was as the clock ran out on my Beth.

No matter what, even when I was sinful, I have always loved and respected God. I have always believed in miracles. It seemed like the only thing I couldn't change or pray my way out of was death. I leafed through my mom's Bible for comfort, reading verses she had underlined:

Set me as a seal upon thine heart, as a seal upon thine arm: *for love is strong as death; jealousy is cruel as the grave*: the coals thereof are coals of fire, which hath a most vehement flame. Many waters cannot quench love, neither can the floods drown it.[4]

"Oh God! I *hate* cancer! I *hate* death! Surely my love for Beth is as strong as death," I cried out. "But death is as cruel as the grave!" I shouted. I cried and prayed and relinquished Beth to God's hands. "O death, where is your sting? O grave, where is your victory?"[5] I quoted and shook my fists. "I can't wait to join forces with Michael and Gabriel so I can kick . . . death's . . . ass!" I thundered.

Then it happened. Beth was gone.

I was in a daze following her death. I don't know if it was shock or grace or what, but somehow, I managed to attend to the details and make it through her funeral in Hawaii. More than thirty million people watched the event—which would have made

Beth very happy. Then we did another smaller memorial service back in Colorado, and the numbness lasted until everybody left. Once it was just me, and I was all by myself, it hit me. *I am all alone!*

This time, I had no small children relying on me to take care of them. I didn't have anyone. I had always given myself fully to the chase—catching the bad guys. Beth had run the business. I didn't know where anything was. I had no idea what state our finances were in. I didn't know who was owed what or how much. I didn't even know what obligations were on my calendar. Every single day, I fought just to make it through that day—to survive.

I went fishing. A lot. It felt good to be outdoors. In nature, I felt God. It was now late August or early September, so the Colorado air was crisp and clean. Breathing it in deeply filled my lungs with life and cleared my head. I took long walks and sat on the bank by the lake, taking in the mountains. I talked to God all the time. I asked Him again and again if Beth was looking down. *Can she see me, Lord?* I was in anguish one minute, at peace the next, and then back to torment.

When I fished, the pain receded into the background for a while. I could focus on baiting the hook. My mind locked in on watching the water; my senses were heightened, waiting to feel the smallest tug on the line for any sign of movement. Then, when I reeled in the fish, took the hook out, and put it on the stringer, my loneliness was less. Even if just for a moment.

I took the dogs with me as I hiked and walked. They were good company, and I talked to them all the time. "Daddy loves you," "It's gonna be okay, guys," "I'm so sorry your mama is not here . . . Daddy tried . . ." and I would break into tears.

Maybe this time, I thought, *it is the end for Dog. Maybe this time, Dog is down for good.*

I had no idea that the heavens were about to open and bring me an incredible gift. Once again, I was about to be given another life.

NINE

DOG'S
NEW DAY

*And the Lord God said, "It is not good that man should
be alone; I will make him a helper comparable to him."*

—Genesis 2:18

"BETH, I WILL NEVER GET MARRIED AGAIN," I TOLD HER, AND I meant it. I first met Beth in 1988, and we were together for many years before we got married in 2006. We had been married for thirteen years. We shared our lives for decades.

"Big Daddy, don't give me that. You are not meant to live alone. You won't make it living alone. You *will* marry again. You have to." She stroked my hair. "Promise me."

As it became clear that Beth's illness was terminal, we had many conversations you wouldn't have with your spouse unless they were dying. But the closer it gets, the more honest you become. No subject was off-limits between us, and Beth made it clear she believed the Lord was taking her out of my life. She knew I had been called to the ministry when I was a kid and said, "When I go, you need a good Christian girl. And you need one that can stand up to you . . . not someone your big personality will overshadow, you hear me?"

I didn't like talking about it. It seemed morbid, and I got emotional whenever she brought it up. I couldn't even bring myself to think about it. I honestly believed after Beth died, I would never marry again. No one could ever take her place. But Beth was right; I was not meant to live alone. On my own, I was depressed. My sadness was heavy, and I started to lose my way. I felt like I had lost my purpose.

I was still under contract with WGN and in need of income—which blew my mind because I thought we had so much more money in the bank than it turned out we did—so I had to finish filming the final episodes of *Dog's Most Wanted* without Beth. It was excruciating. From the very first episode of *Dog the Bounty Hunter*, she had been with me. *How can I do this without her?* I felt hollow inside, and when filming wrapped up, I couldn't wait to get back to Colorado and be with my dogs and go fishing.

A suspicious-looking growth came up on my head. At first, it was just a mild irritation, but it got bigger and became a sore that wouldn't heal. Eventually, I saw a doctor who told me it was likely cancer and I needed to have it removed. "We'll schedule this for tomorrow," he said. "You need to see about this right away."

With Beth's cancer still fresh on my mind and my doctor's serious tone, I knew I better not put it off. *Or should I?* I wondered. *Maybe if I let the cancer eat away at my head until it takes me, I can just go meet my mother, Barbara Katie, and Beth in heaven . . .*

Before I get any further in my story, you need to hear directly from someone else whose story was soon to get woven together with mine. The way God orchestrates things is amazing, and sometimes you need to get multiple perspectives before you can see the big picture. Around the time I was at my lowest—grieving Beth, battling emptiness, and reckoning with the possibility of having cancer myself—a woman named Francie Frane was on a journey of her own. Following is Francie's story in her own words.

"Francie, you have to hear this woman's teachings," Paige said. "You have been struggling so much since Bob died; I think her teaching on healing the wounded soul would really help you."

I didn't think too much about it, but Paige sent me a link to something on YouTube, so I watched it. *Wow!* I thought. *I need more of this!* I looked up Katie Souza's website, called the ministry line, and ordered one of everything!

Ever since my husband Bob had died, I hadn't felt like myself. Life was flat. I was still grieving, and Katie's books and teachings helped me process my grief and begin to heal. Paige and I decided to travel to hear Katie speak in person, and we made our way to Maricopa, Arizona, for a conference. We checked into our hotel and settled into our room. Paige sat on the bed and was scrolling the internet, looking for some worship music to play, when she jumped up and shouted, "Oh my God! Beth Chapman passed away two days ago from cancer!"

"I'm sorry to hear that," I said, "but who is Beth Chapman? Is she a friend?"

Paige looked at me like I was crazy. "Beth Chapman. You know, Dog the Bounty Hunter's wife?"

"Who?" I shook my head and shrugged my shoulders. I had no idea who Dog the Bounty Hunter was. I had never heard of him.

"What—do you live under a rock?" she asked. "I'm sure you've seen him." She pulled up a photo on her phone. "This guy. This is Dog the Bounty Hunter next to his wife, Beth Chapman."

"Paige, I have no idea who he is . . . but he needs a haircut!" I joked.

The next morning, we got up, dressed, and headed to the conference center, where we spent the day with Katie Souza and her team. We worshiped and prayed for hours. It was incredible. It was a small group of people lost in intimate worship with the Lord, and I was soaking it all up.

My friend had a vision. She said, "God is calling you to help abused women. I see you ministering to abused women . . . I can even see you ministering to famous women and helping them get out of abusive relationships. I see you having access to women in Hollywood . . ." Her vision included a black limousine, and she saw Dog the Bounty Hunter helping me out of the car.

"Stop," I told her. I was still processing my grief over losing Bob. I had given my yes to God about my future, but I had some pretty clear ideas about what that yes would look like. It certainly did *not* include a guy whose name was Dog!

"Don't you see?" she said. "You are going to meet Dog the Bounty Hunter. He is going to introduce you to famous women."

"Paige, please!" I said. "That's insane!"

Two months later, I was at home on my Colorado ranch, enjoying my grandson, who spent every other weekend with me. I still had not canceled Bob's cell phone service because occasional business calls came in. I had long since stopped answering it, though. It was almost nine months since Bob had passed away, so if you were calling his phone, you didn't know he had died. I hated giving someone that news.

Invariably, their connection was either so superficial that hearing them say, "Oh, I'm sorry to hear that," was like a knife in my heart, or their friendship was close enough that breaking the news to them meant I ended up having to comfort and console them, which was painful and took precious emotional energy I did not have. I checked the messages now and then to see if there was something important I could not ignore, but most messages I just deleted.

Bob's phone was on the couch next to me, and I saw it blink with a notification that there were voicemail messages. I picked up the phone, sighed, and considered whether I even wanted to check them. I deleted the first message without listening. Then the second. The third message started playing as I tried to drag it into the trash. I couldn't seem to figure out how to make it stop so I could erase it.

A low, gravelly voice said, "This is Doug Chapman. I'm looking for Bob. My next-door neighbor Carlos gave me your number. I need some help with my driveway; I need a good excavator, so if you could give me a call back . . ."

Oh, Carlos! I thought. Carlos was a client of Bob's, and I realized he probably didn't know Bob had passed away. *I should probably tell him*, I thought. *I guess I should call this guy back too.*

I dialed the number from Bob's phone. "Hello," I said, "is Doug there?"

"Who's this?" the raspy voice answered.

"May I speak to Doug, please?" I asked again.

"Who is this?" he countered.

"This is Francie. You left a message for my husband, Bob . . ."

"Yeah, Carlos gave me his number," he answered.

"Well, I'm really sorry, Doug, but Bob passed away a few months ago from cancer."

There was an awkward silence, and then I heard the man start crying.

I just sat there, not sure what to say. *Who is Doug?* I wondered. *And why is he crying over Bob like this?*

The man took a deep breath, then said, "My name's not Doug. It's Dog. Dog the Bounty Hunter . . ." Another pause. ". . . And I just lost my wife to cancer a few months ago."

My jaw dropped, and I started crying. Hearing him say he lost his wife stirred my emotions, and everything Paige said to me in Arizona started playing like a movie in my mind. *Lord, what is happening right now?* I thought.

I stared at the phone and couldn't think of what to say.

"Hello?" he said. "Hello, ma'am, are you there?"

I put the phone back to my ear and said, "I am so, so sorry to hear about your wife. Losing a spouse is the hardest thing I've ever experienced, so I understand what you are feeling right now."

That opened the floodgates, and we talked for almost two hours. We talked about what our spouses had gone through as they got sicker and sicker. We discussed their treatment plans and doctors, our frustration with the medical system, and the high cost of medical bills. We talked about feeling helpless and angry . . . and alone.

Throughout the whole conversation, we poured our hearts out to each other about our spouses, Bob and Beth, and it felt so good to talk to someone who was going through the same thing. I could tell he was in a very low, very dark place, but I also sensed he had a strong faith in God. "Listen," I said, "your life is not over. You can't give up. I know God has a plan for you, and I'm sure your wife would want you to go on living—you have to get back up!" Then I prayed for him.

When I finished, Dog said, "This has to be God because I have talked to several guys who have lost their wives, but no one has talked to me like you are talking to me. No one."

"It's not me," I said. "It's the Holy Spirit. He's the reason we are having this conversation. God knew you needed someone to talk to, and I guess I'm the someone."

"Would you mind if I called you back sometime?" he asked. "I might like to talk to you again."

"Sure," I told him. "When we hang up, I will text you my number. The phone number you called was Bob's, and I don't answer it. It's honestly a miracle I even listened to your voicemail."

"Thanks," he said, "I liked talking to you. I have to go to California, but I would like to call you when I get back."

After we hung up, I called Paige. "Are you sitting down right now?" I asked. "I hope so because you won't believe who I just got off the phone with!" I told her how moved I was by my conversation with Dog the Bounty Hunter and how much we had connected over our grief.

After our call and my friend's vision, I was naturally curious about who he was, so I prayed about it. I felt God directed me not to surf the internet to learn about him. *Trust Me*, I heard God say.

If we are supposed to connect, I prayed, *You will have to orchestrate it. I am not chasing him down.* And I left it at that.

Months went by, then my phone rang at about four o'clock one morning. I reached over and looked at the screen. It was my friend Christina, who was also a widow walking through grief. "Is everything okay?" I asked. "Why are you calling me at this hour? Do you want me to come and pick you up?"

"No!" she said. "This isn't about me—it's about *you*!"

"What are you talking about?" I rubbed my eyes and propped myself up on one elbow. "Calm down, honey; what's really going on?"

"Listen. I was scrolling because I couldn't sleep. I was looking for something to watch from Bethel Music, and a Dog the Bounty Hunter video popped on my screen. I thought, *Bethel Music and Dog the Bounty Hunter, no way! That's too weird.* So I clicked on it."

"Yeah?" I got out of bed and yawned; my brain wanted some oxygen. "What was it about? The interview . . ."

"I'm sending you the video now. You *have to* watch it. Go about four minutes and thirty seconds in and start watching from there. Francie—watch it!" she said, and she hung up.

She texted me a link to an interview with Dog the Bounty Hunter on a local California FOX News station. The interviewer said, "So, Dog, you are about eight months into your grieving process now. You have helped so many people over the years, and I just feel like this—your grief—will become an extension of what you are doing and how you help people."

"Well, Jerry, it's funny you would say that," Dog replied, "because I called this dirt guy, Bob, and his wife, Francie, called me back, and we had this amazing conversation about our grief. I think we really helped each other, and I think maybe God is going to use us together somehow . . ."[1]

I couldn't believe what I was hearing! I watched the whole interview again, then called Christina back. Together we called Paige, who said, "Francie, you have to call him. You have to call him right now!"

But I didn't.

This can't be happening, I rationalized. *This is crazy. I am not calling him!*

About a week later, I shared it with my pastor, who also advised me to call him.

But I didn't.

The following morning, I heard God say, *Call him.*

But I didn't.

This time, though, I did type out a text. That felt safer. Since he was a celebrity, I assumed he likely had women chasing after him all the time, and I did not want to give him the wrong impression. I was certainly not one of those women.

I don't really know you, I texted. I've never watched your show, and I don't want to date you. I am not a fan, but we had this conversation about how there are no coincidences in God's kingdom . . . I think we are supposed to meet.

I stared at the message for a minute, then hit Send.

———————

I woke up that morning missing Beth. It was cold outside. I was not usually up and out this early, and it had just started to snow. The parking lot for the surgical center was nearly empty. There were only three or four cars there when I pulled in. I went inside to the receptionist and got into a room where they came in to have me sign forms and told me it was possible that they might have to take out a piece of my skull. If that happened, they would replace it with a piece of screen.

"What?" I was freaking out. "How bad is this thing? What's going on?" I asked. Flashbacks of Beth getting her cancer diagnosis unleashed anxiety in my body. Blindly, I signed the forms and thought, *Well, if cancer gets me, at least I will get to see my mom and Beth sooner.*

I went through the procedure and had to wait while they biopsied it for the result. My head was killing me, but I took only Tylenol. No matter how much pain I am in, because of my history, I won't take anything stronger than that. I lay there wondering what was next. Finally, the doctor came in and said, "Mr. Chapman, congratulations, it was not cancer. We'll just follow up and keep an eye on it. You're free to go."

I was so relieved. When I walked outside, at least three hundred cars were in the parking lot! I had no idea where my truck was. I walked up and down row after row, the icy wind biting my skin while the snow pelted my bandage. My head was pounding. Within a few minutes, my long hair was frozen back like Jack Frost from the third *Santa Clause* movie.

"This is terrible," I said, and I went back inside and found two security guards. "Excuse me." I tapped the guy on the shoulder. "This is kind of embarrassing, but I can't seem to find my SUV. If I give you boys my keys so you can chirp the lock, would you help me find it?"

"Hey! You're Dog the Bounty Hunter!" one said. "Absolutely, sir, we'll help you find your car."

I stood inside to get warm for a minute, and to my surprise, he came driving my truck up to the door—like full valet service. "Thank you, guys," I said, and I climbed inside and cranked up the heat.

I was almost home when I noticed a two-way radio sitting on the passenger seat. *Oh no!* I thought. *That guy left his radio in my truck! I can't wait until tomorrow; I don't want him to get fired for losing that.* So I turned around and drove all the way back.

On my way home (for the second time), I started feeling sad. Usually, Beth would have been with me for something like I had to do that day. I felt so completely alone. *I can't take it anymore, God!* I prayed, and as I pulled off the side of the road, a scripture came to mind: "What is impossible with man is possible with God."[2]

Am I a pervert if I ask you for a woman, God? It was snowing harder now. It was blanketing everything, making little plops as it landed on my windshield, and the wind swished it around, sounding almost like a broom sweeping a floor. It was not silent, but it was very, very quiet. The falling snow muffled every other sound, and I could hear my own heart beating. I sat in the stillness, waiting to hear God speak. Finally, I got out of the truck, and with the heel of my boot, I carved out a circle in the snow around my vehicle and climbed back inside.

Dear God in heaven, this is sacred ground, I prayed. *Let me see how Adam found Eve. I want to know how You hooked them up.* I didn't have my Thompson Chain-Reference Bible in the truck; I only had my phone, so I started reading Genesis online from the beginning to try to find it. I didn't have to go very far. There it was: "And the LORD God said, 'It is not good that man should be alone; I will make him a helper comparable to him.'"[3]

I had recently started trying to date. It had been so long since I dated that I didn't even really know how to do it anymore. I didn't really even want to date, but I was tired of being lonely. It seemed all the wrong kinds of women were passing me their phone numbers. I wasn't looking for that kind of relationship. I wasn't looking to hook up—I wanted a partner. I was tired of looking. Weary from looking.

God, I prayed, *You brought Eve to Adam. He didn't go looking for her. I am not going to call any of these women back. I am*

going to stop looking. *I will sit back and let You bring me my Eve.*
I want a woman who knows You. I want a woman who is filled
with the Holy Spirit. I want one who can lay hands on the sick
and see them recover. I boldly asked God for a mate, and my faith
started to build. *Lord, I need a woman. In Jesus' name, let's see*
what You do!

Ding. My phone went off, and a text came in from Francie
Frane. I stared at it for at least two minutes. I didn't read it; I just
stared at it. *You know what?* I thought. *I'm going to have coffee*
with this girl. And I don't even drink coffee.

"Hey Francie, I just got your text," I said when she answered
her phone. "I am in the car on my way home from the hospital.
I just had this little procedure done. Hey, do you want to have
coffee with me?"

"Sure," Francie said. "Just coffee, though. This *isn't* a date;
I just thought it might be nice to talk again. How about the
Castle Café?"

We set a time, and I headed in that direction, so I arrived
before she did. I sat in the back of the restaurant, the big bandage
still on my head, and this tall, thin, blond-haired cowgirl walked
in. She wore cowgirl boots, jeans tucked down inside them, a
Western shirt tucked in, and a big belt buckle. It looked like she
was on her way to a rodeo! She walked up to the table. I stood up
and reached for her hand to greet her, and I noticed she had long,
graceful fingers like my mother.

She was a widow and a rancher with hands that reminded me
of my mom. *That's good*, I thought. *Not my type. Off-limits.* As we
visited, she seemed full of the Holy Spirit and talked a lot about
the Bible. I liked her. She was easy to talk to, so I thought I would
connect with her, kind of like a criminal does with their parole

officer. She seemed like someone I needed in my life to keep me on the straight and narrow.

We sat and talked, and I told her about a bounty I was about to go after. It was a man named Lawhead who told me he had carved my name on the brass of his bullet. He was gunning for me. It was a bounty I needed to bring in. If I failed, I would be on the hook for a large sum of money. So I asked Francie to pray for me while I was on that hunt. We finished our coffee "not date" and went our separate ways. I left for LA with Leland to go after Lawhead. I don't mind saying I was a little concerned about this one, and so was Leland.

"Don't worry, son," I said. Then I prayed, *Lord, open his eyes, show him that the hills are full of horses and chariots of fire—there are more with us than against us!* Crouched next to the door, I said, "Leland, get behind your daddy; I'll hit him high; you hit him low." *Boom!* We kicked the door down . . . but we missed Lawhead by mere minutes.

When I returned to my room, I checked my phone. Francie had sent me the scripture from 2 Kings, where Elisha prayed for God to open his servant's eyes to see the horses and chariots surrounding them. That got my attention. *How could she have known that?* I wondered. For the next several weeks, I kept getting random texts from her with scriptures, and every single time it matched something I had seen or thought about that day. We started talking frequently, sometimes for hours until late into the night. I didn't feel lonely when we talked, and our friendship started to grow.

I really enjoy talking to this woman, I thought. We bonded over our grief, and I began to realize that her companionship meant something to me. I called her up and said, "Hey, do you want to go see a movie?" My friend Dwayne "The Rock" Johnson was starring in *Jumanji,* which was a movie where everyone kept their clothes on, and there wasn't too much cussing, so it seemed like a safe pick for a good Christian girl like Francie.

"Well," she said, "I might go see a movie with you if you go to church with me."

I hadn't been inside a church since Beth passed. I called my spiritual advisers occasionally, but I could not bring myself to go to a church service since her funeral. *Maybe this is how God is telling me it is time to get back in church*, I thought. "Uh, okay," I answered, "what kind of church do you go to?"

"Pentecostal," she said.

This wasn't a problem since I grew up in an Assemblies of God church.

"Why don't you come to Friday Night Fire with me?" she asked.

Francie had warned her friends in advance not to do the "celebrity thing" and ask for photos or autographs or anything, and when I arrived, I walked in and saw her sitting all the way near the front in the third row. *Oh, man!* I thought and made my way up the aisle. I was a little late, and the praise service had already started. I slid into the row next to Francie and grabbed her hand, but she pulled hers away, almost flicking mine off.

The music went on for some time, then, as it got quiet, the pastor began praying in tongues. He began, "Shom-mey-dai-cee-tee-tee-ai . . ."

I froze. He said it again. I grabbed Francie's arm and said, "Lady . . ."

"What?" she whispered.

"That's my name in the Spirit—Shom-mey-dai-cee-tee-tee-ai."

Now, I know that might sound strange, but recall that I grew up in a church where people spoke in tongues, and my mother prayed in the Spirit over me every day. When she prayed for me, she uttered those exact same syllables day after day after day. They were burned into my memory. Burned into my spirit. When the pastor spoke in tongues that night, he uttered the same words my mother had, so I knew God was getting ready to speak to me.

The pastor continued praying, only now he was pacing back and forth, his eyes looking over every person in the room. His gaze was intense as he stopped, and his eyes locked with mine. "Dog," he said in a deep, authoritative tone, "come up here!"

My stomach dropped. For a fleeting moment, I considered walking out, but I had too much respect for pastors and too much hunger for God's tangible voice to dare flee the scene. Slowly, I walked toward the platform. I was freaking out on the inside but expectant at the same time. I felt God's presence, something I had not felt in some time. I was ready to come home. It was time to come back to Him—all the way back.

A group of women surrounded me, just like when I was a little boy, and one of them began to prophesy. "Your whole life is about to change. The path that you have been on is not the path that God has for you. God is taking you in a new direction, and what you asked Him for is right in front of you!"

I started shaking.

"You are a warrior," she continued. "God says, 'You are My warrior!'" There was no way this woman could know how often I told God I was His warrior and wanted to fight for Him. When she said this, I knew God was speaking. "Look up!" she said. "God says, what you've asked Me for is standing right in front of you!"

I opened my eyes, and when I looked up, I saw Francie

standing there, both arms raised high. She swayed back and forth slowly as she prayed. I couldn't breathe. I couldn't believe how beautiful she was. All that companionship, the deep friendship we had begun, became a holy attraction. I reached out and grabbed her hand again, but this time, she didn't pull away; she squeezed my hand in hers, and I knew.

We were married on September 2, 2021. A new chapter had begun. I had been given another miracle—God gave me another new chance. One more life.

TEN

DIGGING
UP BONES

And all these blessings shall come upon you and overtake you, because you obey the voice of the Lord *your God.*

—Deuteronomy 28:2

BEFORE I RAN AWAY FROM HOME TO JOIN THE DEVIL'S
Diciples, I stood before the bench in front of Judge Philip Brewster
Gilliam several times for truancy and other crimes. He was the
only juvenile court judge for Denver, and when a minor committed a crime and was convicted, there were two main options for
reform. It was up to the judge where you went. He could send you
to the Gilliam Youth Services Center—basically a strict camp for
bad kids—or he could place you in the Buena Vista Correctional
Facility. This was more like a mini prison for teens, and time
served there was harsh enough to shake you up, make you rethink
your life, straighten up, and fly right.

Judge Gilliam was known for being no-nonsense and notori-
ous for hauling juvenile offenders off to Buena Vista—especially
if he had seen your face in his courtroom before. When Donny
Miller and I got caught mid-robbery with possession of marijuana,
we were not too pleased to find out we would stand before Judge
Gilliam. On the day of my hearing, my lawyer advised me to wear
Levi's jeans and a T-shirt because I would most likely leave the
courtroom and be sent straight to Buena Vista. Donny was up
first, and the judge sentenced him to two years. I guess that was
merciful because he could have given him five.

I watched the bailiff as he took Donny out of the courtroom,
and I don't mind telling you that my stomach was in knots. My
mouth was dry, and I was sweating as Aunt Iris stood behind me
and I went before the judge. To my surprise, the judge did not give

me the same sentence he gave Donny, even though we were both arrested for committing the same crime. "Son, I am going to put you on probation," Judge Gilliam said.

"Probation, Your Honor?" I looked at my aunt Iris in shock. "Thank you!"

"And not only that, but I am also going to suspend that probation unless . . ." He tilted his head down, looking sternly at me over the bench. ". . . *unless* you get in trouble again. Do you understand?"

"Yes, Your Honor, I do." I nodded my head. My knees felt weak.

"Young man, if you change your life, you can end up really being something. Don't get mixed up in this stuff anymore. You have a future ahead of you." He stared at me so hard as he said these words that I felt like his eyes would bore a hole right through me.

———————

My cell phone rang. The display said, "State of Colorado." *Oh no*, I thought, *what do they want? Why are they calling me?*

"You answer it," I said, handing the phone to Francie.

I had been working to help make sure that the penalty for stealing a car in Colorado would remain a felony. I was publicly against the campaign to reduce it to a misdemeanor. I was also vocal about bail reform. As Francie answered the phone, my entire adolescence passed through my mind.

It's been forty-three years, I thought. *Surely the statute of limitations is up for anything they could try to pin on me.* I honestly thought this call was because I had made enemies through my position on felony reduction. I was sure I had made the wrong person angry, and they were trying to get me tangled up and in trouble with the law to keep me quiet.

"This is a private matter," the woman told Francie. "I'm afraid I can speak only with Duane Chapman."

"Okay, well, he'll have to call you back," Francie responded. When she hung up, she convinced me I had to call the woman back. "Dog, it's not like they will just leave you alone if you ignore them. You might as well find out what you're up against."

Reluctantly, I dialed the number, and someone answered and said, "Good afternoon, this is the Colorado Department of Public Health and Environment. How may I direct your call?"

I gave the receptionist my name and the woman's name who had just spoken with Francie, and they transferred me to her.

"Is this Duane Chapman?" she asked.

"Yes," I answered, "may I ask what this is about?"

"Do you remember a girl named Sharon Michelle Waters?" she asked.[1] "Did you know her?"

"Yes?" I answered cautiously. I hadn't heard her name in decades. She had been my first legitimate girlfriend. Of course I remembered her.

"Sir, a few years ago, in 2016 to be exact, Colorado passed a law that opened access to original birth certificates for adoptees. This means children who were part of a closed adoption can now find out who their birth parents are. Do you follow me?"

"Sure," I said.

Wow, I thought. *I guess Sharon must have had a baby and needs help locating the child.*

As Dog the Bounty Hunter, I get calls to help track down lost people all the time, so I was eager to help Sharon if I could.

I asked the woman, "Well, are we looking for a boy or a girl? Do you have any information about their last known address?" I began to ask her the kinds of questions that helped me get started on a hunt.

"Sir," she interrupted, "the birth record shows that the father is *Duane Lee Chapman*, and the mother is listed as Sharon Michelle Waters."

I still didn't make the connection. I had no memory of Sharon being pregnant.

"Ms. Waters had a baby when she was sixteen, and she listed you as the father on the child's birth certificate," she continued. "It looks like you have a son, Mr. Chapman."

My mind raced, searching for memories. *Had Sharon been pregnant when we were together?* I was her first boyfriend, and she was my first girlfriend. We were kids. We were so young and so naive; I'm not sure we even really knew that much about sex then. I mostly took her to church with me. I struggled to locate the memories. And this was not the first time someone had come out of the woodwork to claim I was their father. As a celebrity, it happens more often than you might think. I found out about Christopher that way, but with a few others who claimed I was their dad, a DNA test proved their claim was false.

Finally, I said, "Okay." I had no idea how long I had paused. "Can I get his number?"

"I'm afraid that's not possible until you sign paperwork that permits me to share your information with him. Would you be willing to submit to a DNA test?" she asked.

"Absolutely," I said. "Is he willing to get one?"

"He has already taken one," she said. "He is eager to find his birth parents. So I will send the paperwork over for you to sign, and after you get your test done, we'll submit them both to our lab for DNA matching."

I hung up the phone and explained the call to Francie.

She said, "Well, you keep telling me you wish we could have a baby together, and *that's* certainly not going to happen. If this boy turns out to be your son, we'll just count him as ours!"

I waited for what felt like an eternity. Finally, I couldn't handle the suspense any longer. I called the lady from social services and asked if I could please have the boy's number; I wanted to talk to him. I learned from social services that they had shown him a copy of his birth certificate with the parents' names blurred out. He could see he was born in Denver, Colorado, and he could see the birthdates of Sharon and me. So he at least had clues, which was more than I had. "Please, ma'am," I said, "put me out of my misery, and let me reach out to the boy."

My mind was filled with questions, and I couldn't wait to talk to him. Reluctantly, she gave me his number. I called him up and said, "Hello, is this John?"

"This is John," he said. "Who is this?"

"Who do you think I am?" I asked.

He had me on speaker and said, "I'm not sure."

"Come on, who do you think this is?" I teased.

He hesitated. "Are you Dog?"

"No," I said.

"Are you Steven Van Zandt from *The Sopranos*?"

"What? No," I said, but now I was laughing. "I'm kidding. John, this is Dog the Bounty Hunter."

"I knew it!" shouted the woman with him. "I could tell it was you from your voice! I knew your dad was Dog the Bounty Hunter!"

"What made you think that?" I asked.

"Because he looks just like you—and your birthday matches the birth certificate. I *knew* John's dad was somebody famous!" she exclaimed.

She introduced herself as Jodie, and John and I talked for a few minutes. I really liked him. I hadn't seen a photo of him yet, so I had no idea what he looked like. I didn't even know where he lived or what he did for a living, but he seemed so genuine about wanting to connect to his biological parents; it moved me.

"Listen," I said, "I have had a few of these calls in my day, and that's why I wanted a DNA test—to make sure. But even if it turns out that I'm not your dad, I want you to know you can call me Dad."

"Thanks," he said. "Wow. That means so much."

A few weeks passed, and the woman from social services finally called me back. "Mr. Chapman," she began, "I don't know if I should say I'm sorry or congratulations. Are you sitting down?"

"No, ma'am, I would rather take the news standing up." But my heart sank. I felt like she was going to tell me the DNA didn't match, and I already felt an attachment to John.

"Mr. Chapman, the DNA result shows a 98.99 percent match. There is no mistake; that's your boy."

"No!" I shouted. Then I started crying. I hung up and called out to Francie, "I have another son! Francie, did you hear that? I have another boy!" I was so excited. I had to call John right away.

He picked up the phone. "Hi, Dad!" He already knew.

"Oh my God—John, I am so happy to find out you are my boy. Man, I would really love to come see you. Could we do that?" I asked.

"Well, I'm pretty glad to hear you say that," he said, "because

Jodie and I are just outside of Castle Rock, and I am already on my way to see you!"

After he hung up, I hugged Francie and said, "We got a baby together after all. Now *we* have a baby—you and me!"

It turns out this boy—child number thirteen—was my first-born child. I wore the number 13 on my jacket for years, and that number has always held special meaning for me. "So the last will be first, and the first last,"[2] I quoted. I was so curious about him. Who was he? What did he look like? When was his birthday? Would he like me? My anticipation of meeting him grew.

I sent him a text to meet us for dinner at 7:30, and Francie and I got to the restaurant early. At 7:20, John responded, Sorry. I just got your text. We are running a little late.

I sent back, That's okay; get here as soon as you can. Let me know when you are five minutes out so my guy can put a microphone on you. Nick is my top camera guy, and he is going to film us meeting for the first time.

I am so used to having our whole lives caught on film, I didn't think about how strange that might have sounded to John and Jodie.

———————

I stared at the copy of the birth certificate, willing my memories to surface. I wondered what kind of trauma must have surrounded the situation for my brain to block off any memory of Sharon being pregnant. I would never have run off to Phoenix if I had known. I struggled to work out the math of when I had last seen her and when I ran away from home, but all the details were fuzzy.

Then my thoughts went to her. What kind of trauma must she have been through to be pregnant at such a young age? I thought back to the people from my Assemblies of God church and how they talked about unwed mothers. The only thing they ever taught us about sex was that it was a sin. Being pregnant out of wedlock was considered shameful. It was the kind of thing people kept secret. Pregnant girls were kicked out of school. They went to live with relatives and hid away until after they gave birth. *Oh, Sharon, I am so sorry,* I thought.

My heart went out to her. I couldn't imagine how hard it must have been to be pregnant so young. To have a baby before you even finished high school. I felt so guilty that I hadn't known. *She must have felt so alone. A closed adoption?* I thought. That must have meant even her parents didn't want to help her. *It must have been so hard to go through. Giving up a baby and never knowing what became of him—I don't think I could have done it.*

Then I thought about John growing up knowing he was adopted. *I wonder when he found out? What was it like for him not knowing who his biological mother and father were?* I thought about my own dad—my stepdad—and how he treated me. He knew I wasn't his boy the whole time, and I always questioned if his abuse was his way of taking that anger out on me. So I wondered about John's adoptive dad. *Did John have a father figure who treated him well, or was it more like me and my dad?*

I searched my memories of the time surrounding when I had run away from home. I remembered riding my chopper all the way from Denver to Phoenix with Ray-Ray from the Hades Heads, another outlaw biker club. I had just quit school in the seventh grade. I looked so young that we forged a letter saying that Ray Sexton was my legal guardian so I wouldn't get into trouble.

I vividly remembered walking out of the school. I remembered riding away from Denver, wind in my face, troubles at my back, but I could not recall one memory of Sharon being pregnant. I also couldn't remember how or when we broke up either. *When was the last time I saw her?* I loved her. When I told my parents I loved Sharon, my dad had said, "That's just puppy love, boy." But my mom defended me, saying, "Wesley, it's real to the puppy." I loved her as much as anyone is capable of love at fifteen. After I ran away to Phoenix, I didn't contact anyone in my family for more than a year, so who knows what trauma had trapped what memories and buried them out of my reach to recall.

I looked down at the birth certificate again, and an electric shock went through my body. Two things stood out to me. The first was that this baby boy was born on June 26, 1971. *June 26* jumped out at me like a neon sign. Beth had passed away on June 26. Tears started to flow. Since Beth's death, that date had haunted me. Each year as it came up on the calendar, I was caught up in fresh grief. I dreaded that day. Hated it.

Now, here was redemption. My firstborn son was born on June 26. I now had a reason to celebrate the day instead of mourning it. As Jesus had promised His disciples would happen after His death, God had turned my sorrow into joy.[3]

The second was who had signed the birth certificate—Judge Philip Gilliam.

When I stood in front of the judge that last time, did he know I had a son? Did he show me mercy because he had seen this adoption certificate with my name on it? The judge has long since left this earth, and my memories of the timeline are too fuzzy to figure it out for sure, so I guess I'll never know the answer to that question. But Judge Gilliam had been a huge part of my life as an adolescent. His signature on the bottom right-hand corner of my son's birth certificate hit me like a ton of bricks. I felt the significance, even if I couldn't explain it.

I gripped Francie's hand tightly, waiting for John and Jodie to enter the restaurant. When they walked through the door, I jumped to my feet, and we all hugged each other. Jodie was pretty. She had big hair like my Francie and wore the biggest, most beautiful smile. I searched John's face for my features, and I could see the resemblance between him, Duane Lee, Leland, and Christopher. We were all nervous and excited and talked on top of each other, asking question after question.

I learned he had been to prison young—just like his old man—and had loved the gang life up until he had children and realized he wanted something better for them.

"You were a boxer? No way!" I exclaimed.

"Yeah, I was a pro boxer until '91," John said.

"So was I . . . and Leland too. I guess boxing is in our blood, boy!"

On and on we went, making discoveries about each other. I learned John had not had a good relationship with his adoptive dad, and some of his early childhood experiences were like mine in that regard. He has three children and three grandchildren—which meant I have three more grandchildren and three great-grandchildren—and he clearly loved Jodie. His family meant everything to him, so that was like me too.

"Can I ask what made you want to find your biological parents?" Francie said.

"Sure," he said. "When I was about twelve or so, I found out I was adopted. It kind of made sense to me because I never really felt like I fit. Deep down, I always thought I didn't belong there with them. I didn't know why I felt that way; I just did. I didn't think about trying to find my parents until my early twenties. It was like I had puzzle pieces, but I didn't know how they fit together. I had lots of questions: Why am I like this? Who am I? Where did I really come from? Why was I put up for adoption? And lots of other questions I just wanted answers to."

I sighed and gripped Francie's hand. She had also been adopted, so she had prepared me for the kind of struggle John had faced as a child. She also knew what it was like to feel that you didn't belong and have so many unanswered questions. "I'm so sorry, son," was all I could think of to say.

"You looked for your dad in your twenties? But you are fifty now. What happened?" Francie asked.

"Yeah, I was on my own back then. I didn't have any help, but I wanted to find out. I learned from my adoptive mom what hospital I was born in, so I traveled back to Denver and went to the hospital records room, but I hit a dead end. At that time, a law prevented kids in a closed adoption from learning the details of their birth, so I figured that was it."

"But in 2016," Jodie interrupted, "a law was passed that let kids be able to see their birth records. We contacted the State of Colorado to ask, but they couldn't find John's. Colorado is a long way from Iowa, so we were stuck trying to do everything over the phone. We never even got to talk to the same person twice anytime we called, so it was like starting over every time."

"Then, a few months ago," John continued, "Jodie decided to try again. It had been a few years since the law first passed, so I guess they got more efficient about handling requests like ours. Jodie got hold of a woman who directed her to the county courthouse, and they did a records search."

Jodie said, "The woman called us back much faster than we expected, and she told John they found his birth certificate! When John asked her what his parents' names were, she said, 'I can't tell you yet until we contact them, but I can tell you that your dad is kind of famous.'"

"Oh my gosh," Francie said, "they told you they knew but couldn't tell you! That must have been so frustrating!"

"It was!" Jodie said. "I kept asking, 'Who is it?' and saying, 'I want to know!' but John was pretty quiet. I think he was just processing that his parents had just been found after all this time."

John nodded. "The woman told us they couldn't release any of the information to me until you and my birth mother both signed a form, but she did give us a few hints. She told us your birthday was February 2, 1953, and she said you were a tough guy and gave us a few other clues."

"When did you guess it was me?" I asked.

"Jodie always told me she thought my dad was somebody famous. We googled famous people born on your birthday, and a photo came up of you in your forties, wearing sunglasses, and Jodie said, 'He looks just like you!' But I wasn't as sure."

"He talks like you!" Jodie said. "And some of his mannerisms and the way he looks from the side—it was uncanny. So I was sure you were his dad."

We kept talking, learning about and getting to know each other better. I just kept thinking, *Whoa, this kid is a chip off the old block!* and I wanted to know him more. I wanted to know him as my son, and I wanted him to know me as his father.

I learned John loved the outdoors and fishing. He had also gotten into trouble as a teen—stealing things for the adrenaline rush. When he was seventeen, he stood before a judge to be tried as an adult. He was there asking for a bond reduction, and the judge had said, "Son, you have the record of a forty-year-old career criminal. Bond denied." That was his turning point. He thought about his kids and the impact it would have on them if he were in jail, so he got himself together and eventually opened his own construction business.

An entrepreneur—just like his old man!

"Happy birthday to you, happy birthday to you. Happy birthday, dear Do-og, happy birthday to you!" Francie sang to me as she came into our room. She crawled into bed next to me and snuggled close. "What would you like for your birthday?" she asked.

"This," I said, and I squeezed her tight. "I have absolutely everything my heart desires."

She kissed me, and when she pulled away, she had that twinkle in her eyes. "Well, I might have something here to make your day a little more special," she teased, holding out an envelope. It was from John. This was my first birthday since meeting him, and I took the envelope from Francie with anticipation.

"From John?" I asked, looking at the return address.

"From John," she said. "Open it; maybe he sent you a card!"

I tore the envelope open, touched that he had thought about my birthday. In the envelope was a copy of John's new driver's license. Next to his photo, his name was printed as John Allen Chapman.

"Francie!" I said. "Look at this!" And I handed the license copy to her. "He changed his name! My boy changed his name to mine!"

It was the best birthday present! A son I never knew existed had searched for me. And when he found me, instead of being angry that I had not been part of his life, he accepted me. He had embraced me as his father and was so happy to belong to my family that he legally changed his name to Chapman. John Allen Chapman, son of Duane Lee Chapman.

"Thank You, God," was all I could say. This miracle was a gift I had not asked for. God had given me a blessing I did not even seek. *Why, God?* I asked. *Why did You bring John to me?*

"And all these blessings shall come upon you and overtake you, because you obey the voice of the Lord your God,"[4] He answered. *"Just like I told the Israelites in Deuteronomy. When you obey Me, I bless you. You set your heart toward Me when you rededicated your life, and John is My blessing to you. Receive your son."*

I cried.

Life with Francie was clearly going to be an adventure. This was a new chapter for me. I am the same man, but I am also a new creation. I walked outside with John's paper still in my hand. I looked down at his name and smiled. I breathed in the cool morning air and looked out at the horizon. *What do You have in store for me, God? What's next for the Dog?*

ELEVEN

DOG'S
NEXT HUNT

"Here am I! Send me."

—Isaiah 6:8

I AM DOG THE BOUNTY HUNTER. I WILL ALWAYS BE DOG THE Bounty Hunter. Until the day I cannot physically chase down bad guys, you can be sure I will be out there on the hunt! In the last forty years, I have chased down and caught more than ten thousand people, and that's a record I believe will stand. But these days, I am no longer going after bail jumpers. I don't get interested in chasing people unless they are felons and either the boys in blue or the Feds in black can't seem to track them down to bring them to justice.

I don't care where the chase leads me. I will hunt them down wherever they hide! I am especially motivated if the criminal on the run is accused of harming a woman or a child. When I hear about a crime like this, my inner warrior rises up, and I can't help it—I have to join the hunt to find him and take him down! I feel the cry of the innocent for justice.

It makes me remember the story of Cain and Abel in the Bible when Cain killed his brother in jealous anger. God asked Cain, "Where is your brother, Abel?" and he answered, "I don't know; I'm not his keeper." But God told him that his brother's blood cried out to Him from the ground.[1] It's the same with me. It's as if the blood of the victim cries out to me from the ground. I must go.

Because Beth was such an important part of my television success as Dog the Bounty Hunter and fans still have a deep connection to her, some have criticized or questioned whether I should continue bounty hunting with Francie as my wife. Some have even suggested it is time for me to hang up my badge, but I can't do that. I will always honor Beth's memory, and I am grateful for the life we had together. I still grieve her passing, as Francie does for Bob. As a widower and a widow, we will never forget the spouses we lost, but Francie married me as Duane "Dog" Chapman—Dog the Bounty Hunter. She knew when she said yes that hunting down bad guys to bring them to justice is an important part of who I am. It's in my blood.

This was confirmed shortly following our wedding. Within days of our ceremony, people started reaching out to me about the search for Brian Laundrie after the body of his fiancée, Gabby Petito, was found in the Grand Tetons and the case gained national attention. I am a father. I lost Barbara Katie when she was twenty-three, so I had an immediate emotional connection with Gabby's parents.

I always say the bigger the case, the more information you have because people are curious. They pay attention, and they are excited to share what they know. They may not be able to chase him, but they gladly give us their tips to help us. People want justice served, so they get invested and want the guy found.

We were on the first night of our honeymoon in Florida. After Francie was sound asleep, I got up and googled to find out how far Laundrie's family home was from where we were staying. I couldn't help my curiosity. I couldn't believe it—their house was only about a hundred miles from the beach where we were staying! *Only a hundred miles*, I thought.

I sat there staring at the screen, wrestling with my urge to go after Laundrie because I knew a honeymoon was about connecting with your spouse. For me, it is about spoiling your bride and making sure she has the time of her life and knows how excited you are to be with her. I didn't want to spoil our honeymoon by being distracted by the hunt for Brian Laundrie. I approached Francie cautiously, gently woke her up, and said, "Hi, baby. Say, do you realize that our hotel is only a hundred miles from the house where Brian Laundrie's parents live?"

I sat there on the edge of the bed and said nothing. Waiting. I had already decided if Francie was not intrigued by it or if she just wanted to go sit on the beach, then I would honor her and stay out of the hunt until after our honeymoon was over. We had chosen Florida because Francie wanted to play in the ocean and put her feet in the sand. But she surprised me. She got this twinkle in her eyes, broke into a big smile, and said, "Honey, do you want to go there?"

"So bad," I answered.

"Okay," she leaned over and kissed me, "let's go tomorrow." God, I love that woman!

We took a road trip just to do a drive-by of the house and neighborhood. I wanted to get the lay of the land. Sometimes when I see a place, I hear God talk to me about the person, and He gives me something—a clue—that helps me locate them.

I don't mind telling you that I was a little worried about confronting Laundrie's father. You could see from press interviews that he was aggravated and on edge. Florida has a Stand Your Ground law that allows you to shoot someone in self-defense. So if I approached Mr. Laundrie at his home and he perceived I was a threat, according to the state of Florida, he could shoot me without legal repercussions.

Francie and I had been married only a short time, and I was in no hurry to exit earth, but I felt like I had to prove to my new wife that I was a brave man. *If he shoots me*, I rationalized, *at least Francie will see me go down in a blaze of glory!*

When we found the neighborhood, I could see reporters everywhere. We drove past the house a few times, and on my third trip around the block, a cop waved me over.

"Hello, Officer," I said, rolling down my window. "How are you?"

"Hey! You're Dog the Bounty Hunter!" he exclaimed.

"Yes, sir, I am. I've been driving around this neighborhood thinking about Brian Laundrie. That's his parents' house, right? I would really like to go up there and knock on the door."

"Well, when do you want to go?" he asked.

"Right now," I bluffed. I expected him to tell me I couldn't. With so many reporters around, I was sure there had to be an injunction against the press bothering them for interviews or something, but I didn't want to let Francie down.

"Hang on," he said, "let me pull my officers off the door first."

"What?" I answered, surprised. "Oh no, that's okay . . ."

"Yeah, yeah! Let's go up there!" Francie shouted.

"Honey, reporters are crawling all over the place. If Laundrie is in there, he is not coming out, and his family is certainly not going to let me in!" I protested. "I probably need to scout the area more so I can come up with a plan. Maybe we should come back later when they let their guard down."

"Well, we drove all this way. Aren't you at least gonna knock?" she asked.

"Baby . . ."

But she had that look in her eyes, which I already knew meant I was going to go knock on that door. We parked, and I walked up the driveway and approached the front door.

"That's Dog the Bounty Hunter!" I could hear reporters shouting. It looked like cockroaches with cameras climbing out of hedges and over rooftops, coming out from behind cars.

This is nuts, I thought as I approached the front entrance. *He could still shoot me.* The house had one of those metal storm doors with a screen that you could keep shut while the main door was open so you could let in a breeze. I banged loudly. My signature knock.

No answer.

I walked around and then banged again.

No response.

I knocked several times, with my every move caught on camera. If you search, you will find video footage all over the internet from several major news outlets that captured me walking up to the Laundries' house, banging on the door (without any answer), and talking to the neighbors across the fence.

I felt in my gut the parents knew where their son was. Whether they wanted to talk to me or not, I could just feel that Laundrie was close.

"He's near," I told Francie as I slid back into the car. "That boy slunk back home with his tail between his legs, and I'm going to find him for Gabby's parents—for Gabby!"

As we drove off, I said, "Well, Dog the Bounty Hunter knocking on his door is going to rain down attention on this family. This thing just got lit up!"

That evening when we got back, I started researching the case more. I found an article titled "The Knock Heard Around the World." I was so proud of that! I knew that my interest and involvement meant national media attention would swell. That was good for the case because the more media coverage, the more average citizens would be on the lookout and have valuable information.

Our tip line got thousands of calls. I had put together a team I call "The Essentials," made up of retired law enforcement officers and federal agents still in their prime whose wisdom and experience are too good to waste.

In the weeks that followed knocking on the door, we tracked down a lot of clues. We followed up with Laundrie's sister and brother-in-law. We followed the trail to the Myakkahatchee Creek Environmental Park, where we found evidence from license plate recognition that the Laundrie family's truck and camper had been there. We knew we were getting close, and we were certainly helping to put the pressure on.

Then one morning around seven, the parents suddenly decided to go looking for Brian . . . in that same park where we knew the Laundries had already been. Not long after, the news broke that human skeletal remains, along with Brian Laundrie's backpack and a notebook, had been found in an area previously searched by law enforcement. The news reported that the area had been underwater earlier, and the water had now receded. Later, the case summary from the medical examiner tasked with investigating Laundrie's death noted that the area had been under approximately three feet of water, based on water-line evidence on nearby trees.

However, when I talked with a group of Native Americans living nearby, they told me the water had receded only about an inch in two months, so a body or a backpack should still have been visible to someone searching. But it was Mr. Laundrie who led the FBI to the spot. He took them down a trail inside a 160-acre tree-filled park inside the 25,000-acre Carlton Reserve, where he soon stumbled upon items belonging to his son.

You read that right. Mr. Laundrie almost immediately found his son's backpack—off-trail—inside a 160-acre swampy, tree-filled park in a 25,000-acre nature reserve, leading quickly to the subsequent discovery of his son's skeletal remains.[2]

I believe in miracles, but that seems miraculous indeed!

The Laundrie family attorney described this remarkable feat as "happenstance."[3] The public was asked to believe that this incredible discovery that had eluded the skilled search teams with state-of-the-art resources from the FBI and sheriff's departments had been made by an amateur tracker.

On top of that, among the items found was a paper notebook with a legible, handwritten note confessing to the murder of Gabby Petito. The notebook was located "outside of the dry bag"[4] in a wooden box in an area that was supposed to have been under-water for a month.

It wasn't a watertight box, just a regular wooden box.

Imagine this: Take a paper notebook and write in it. Put that notebook inside a wooden jewelry box, then drop that box in a swimming pool and leave it underwater for a month. Then pull the box out of the water and retrieve the notebook. What do you think the odds are that the paper has not disintegrated or that a note you wrote on that paper would still be legible? Even if the notebook had been inside the white plastic bag found, it seems far-fetched to me.

And a person in the state of mind to commit suicide seems unlikely to think, *I am about to kill myself inside a swamp; I guess I better seal up this suicide confession in a watertight bag so when they find my body, they can still read it.* To me, it just didn't add up.

Because of the state of the remains, dental records were used for initial identification. That was followed soon after by DNA verification, and Laundrie's death was ruled a suicide. The autopsy report concluded Laundrie shot himself in the left side of his head with a .38. This is a curious finding since Brian was right-handed.[5] It does not follow the usual pattern of suicide by a gunshot.

The whole thing felt suspect to me. The case was closed, but it bothered me. So I did what I always do; I talked to God about it. When I went after Andrew Luster, God gave me a clear answer when I asked about pursuing him into Mexico. This time, however, God did not give me a clear confirmation. I felt like He told me not to be lazy and to do more investigation. To dig deeper.

The sheriff asked, "Dog, are you done with this case?"

"I don't know," I answered.

"Well, the only way someone can outrun you is to die!" he said.

I have wrestled with this one. To this day, I believe there are too many irregularities and inconsistencies that have not been explained satisfactorily. Officially, the case is closed, but I feel like we don't have all the answers.

I share my story about the Laundrie hunt with you for two reasons:

1. It still feels like unfinished business to me. I didn't get the chance to find him before his case was officially closed.
2. Francie's partnership with me on that first hunt after our wedding confirmed that she was cut out for bounty hunting by my side. She was a natural, and I was overjoyed!

God brought me a woman who loves me as I am and who expects me to grow to become everything I can be. As committed as she is to chasing down bad guys with me, she is even more committed to chasing after God with me. Before I met Francie, my relationship with God had been off and on. I always went to Him in desperation or trouble, and I went to Him for help tracking down criminals.

A fair bit of my prayers have been spent "making deals" with God because I read the story in the book of Exodus where Moses came down the mountain with the Ten Commandments and caught the Israelites worshiping the golden calf. God was so angry that He told Moses He would destroy the people because of their disobedience. But after God and Moses had a conversation, God changed His mind and didn't do it.[6] I believed if Moses could get God to change His mind, I could too. I know God loves me as much as He loved Moses.

Even when I did sinful things and was not walking right with God, I still shared about Jesus with those who needed His love and guidance. I have never been ashamed of my faith, and I was never ashamed to tell people about Jesus. After I met Francie and saw how her relationship with God was a daily thing, I realized that I went to God mostly for things I needed or wanted. I was not in the habit of just spending time with Him. I went to God when I was low, but I didn't go to God when I was happy. I do now!

I intend to keep on chasing down bad guys as Dog the Bounty Hunter. When I find them to bring them to justice, I will keep giving them the backseat treatment of mercy and letting them know God gives them a chance to turn their life around. I will always love doing television, and I will gladly take on acting roles and do more reality TV. I will use whatever platform God gives me access to and whatever influence that brings to name-drop for Jesus.

As a child, it was prophesied over me that I would preach the gospel to millions. I don't feel a calling to preach in churches. I feel a calling to preach in the streets. My life is my message. I want to share God's light and love with people who won't go inside a church. My life as Dog the Bounty Hunter has been spoofed on *The Simpsons*, *Family Guy*, *South Park*, and more than a dozen other shows that are not remotely Christian. Yet even in *South Park*, arguably one of the most crass cartoons out there, the guy spoofing my character says, "Go with Christ, brah."[7]

So, like Paul, I rejoice that Christ is being preached by whatever means it happens. I may not stand on a platform behind a pulpit on Sunday mornings, but my success as a bounty hunter and entertainer with my trademark mullet, feathers, sunglasses, and badge has given me a platform to talk about Jesus to people who need to know He loves them.

A chief once told me, "Dog, it's always dark before the light. And people believe a lie until the truth is told."

I know that Jesus is the truth and the light. I carry His truth, and I am His light.

Light belongs in dark places.

Francie and I know we are called to bring light to dark places. I carry my light to the streets. Francie carries her light to the victims of the street.

Using the platform of my fame, Francie started Light Up the Darkness Ministries, dedicated to helping the brokenhearted and victims of domestic violence, sexual abuse, and trafficking. She is passionate about this ministry's mission. Together with Katie Souza, Francie set up the D.O.G. Foundation—Developing an Overcoming Generation—and established Dog's House of Bounty to provide victims with safe housing, counseling, life-skills training, soul-healing, and other intervention services. They have an eighteen-month program to help women recover and get restored, to regain their identity and power.

That goes even further than the "backseat treatment" I became famous for on TV. House of Bounty is on a whole new level. I am humbled my name is attached to it, and I am grateful to Francie for all her work with the ministry and to her and Katie for their efforts with the foundation.

As a bounty hunter, catching my man means a paycheck. Collecting the bounty is my reward. But these days, I think a lot less about silver and gold. If I capture a person's soul with my story, and they give their life to Christ, there is no greater prize. Giving God glory is my reward. I have caught ten thousand criminals in my lifetime. Now I am asking God for ten thousand souls for His kingdom.

I named this book *Nine Lives and Counting* for a reason. It's not just because I have had so many close calls and dangerous moments with criminals. It is because God's mercies are new every morning.[8] I have shared some of my major highs and major lows with you. Each time I feel like I have messed things up beyond all repair, God has given me the miracle of another chance to walk in faith and redemption. He has given me a chance at another life.

1. Life as a boy, growing up in church
2. Life in a biker gang, chasing my own pursuits
3. Life in a maximum-security prison, doing time as a felon
4. Life after prison, selling vacuum cleaners to make ends meet and trying to get custody of my boys

5. Life as a bounty hunter, living as a single dad, meeting Tony Robbins, deciding to move to Hawaii, and then losing my mother

6. Life after moving back to Colorado, connecting with Beth and moving back to Hawaii, the high-profile capture of Andrew Luster, and becoming a reality television star

7. Life after losing my daughter Barbara Katie and overcoming that grief as I began my marriage to Beth

8. Life after a scandal that almost took me down, our miraculous comeback, working with two more television networks, and walking through Beth's cancer

9. Life after losing Beth, healing from grief, and meeting Francie

10. . . . and counting!

Through it all, the one constant has been my faith in God. He has never left me or forsaken me. He has always been there, ready to hear me when I call. He has given me so many new chances. With all my heart, I want you to know God and give Him your life too.

Dog's next hunt is for you.

TWELVE

DOG'S
INVITATION

"Lord, remember me . . ."

—Luke 23:42

I RELATE MORE AND MORE TO KING DAVID EVERY DAY. I UNDER-stand David as a warrior. I understand him as a guy who was part of a conspiracy to commit murder and an accessory after the fact. I understand him as an adulterer. I understand David as a guy who fought the Philistines with his bare hands and passionately chased after the enemies of God's people. I understand him as a man who worshiped God with all his might. I understand him as a man with complicated relationships with his children, and I understand him as a man who watered his couch with his tears when he was in grief.

My mother often told me as a child that I was a little David. She told me God loved David because he was so good at repent-ing, and I needed to be good at repenting too. I pray all the time to ask God to forgive me of my sins. Like David, I pray, "Create in me a clean heart, O God; and renew a right spirit within me. Cast me not away from thy presence; and take not thy holy spirit from me."[1]

David was known as a man after God's own heart. Man, I want to be known like that too.

Every day I pray and ask God to forgive me for specific sins I know I have done. I also ask Him to forgive me for sins I didn't even know I committed. Those kinds of sins are called *trespasses*, and they are just like that—like going inside a building when you don't see a No Trespassing sign. You didn't know it was wrong when you did it. I repent like this every day. Why? I never know if today is my last day on earth, and when I meet God, I want to walk into heaven with clean hands and a pure heart. I want to meet Him as a forgiven man, washed clean by the blood of the Lamb.

Sometimes I meet someone who feels like they have gone too far. They feel like they have committed so many sins—or maybe just the really bad ones—that they are beyond hope. But that isn't true. If you still have enough of a conscience to recognize that you have been sinful and have any curiosity about God inside you, you haven't gone too far. God can and will forgive you.

When you ask for forgiveness, the Bible says He throws your sins into the sea of forgetfulness.[2] For example, say you shoplift, and you ask God to forgive you for shoplifting. The next time you go to Him, if you say, "Remember when I talked to You about shoplifting?" He'll say no. When God forgives you, He removes that sin from you as far as the east is from the west.[3]

I am no theologian. I am not a pastor or even a preacher, but I am a forgiven man! So let me ask you, how far is the east from the west, friend? You don't need to bring that thing up with God ever again. Once you confess sin and ask God to forgive you, it's over. Done. Not guilty.

This Dog's been pardoned!

I have personally experienced the mercy of God and His forgiveness. At the foot of the cross, we are all equal. Sin is sin. We are the ones who decide which sins are more socially acceptable than others. The murderer is the same in God's eyes as the church lady who gossips.

When you ask God to forgive you and live inside you as Lord, you don't have to suffer the sentence you deserve for all the bad things you have done. Jesus took that punishment for you. You are God's child. Jesus becomes your brother, and heaven is your home.

That's good news.

I am God's messenger, and I carry this message to you. I want you to know that you can be forgiven. All you have to do is ask.

Maybe you know you need God's forgiveness. Maybe your life is a mess, and you could really use His help. Maybe you are hungry for His love. Maybe you don't believe God cares about you or aren't even sure if He is real.

Think about this: If I am wrong and God is not real, you've got nothing to lose. But if I'm right and God is who He says He is, then you could lose everything by not believing. Why not give this a shot?

Maybe you haven't prayed in a long time—or ever. Maybe you aren't even sure how to pray. Maybe you think you have to do something first to get cleaned up enough to talk to God.

But you don't.

You can come to God exactly as you are right now. There is nothing you need to do first. All you have to do is believe.

That's all. Believe that God sent His Son, Jesus, to pay the penalty for your sin—Jesus went to prison in your place so you could know God. That's His gift to you—salvation. Jesus does the saving, brother; all we do is the asking.

And I have more good news. You don't have to go inside a church, walk down an aisle, or shake a preacher's hand to receive Jesus. You can do it right now, wherever you are. You just have to ask Him to come and live in your heart.

If you are still breathing, then it's not too late.

A friend of mine lost his dad recently. His father wasn't a particularly nice man. He was an alcoholic and hadn't been much of a father. But in his final days, he repented and asked Jesus to save him. My friend asked me, "Dog, my dad lived such a bad life for so many years. Do you mean to tell me that his confession at the very end was enough? I need to know—is my dad in heaven?"

"Yes," I said confidently. "If your dad accepted the Lord before he died, he is in heaven. There is no doubt in my mind. It is never too late."

"That's a relief," my friend said, and he let out a big sigh.

"It sure is," I said. "How about you? If you died today, would you see your dad in heaven?"

"I'm not sure," he answered.

"Well, I know how to make sure," I said, and we prayed together for him to accept Christ.

"Now, if your son ever calls me and has to ask if you went to heaven, I'll be able to tell him yes, brother!" I hung up that phone smiling.

Prayer is easy. It is just talking to God, and God's mercy is big enough to handle and cover anything you have ever done. There is nothing so bad that it can disqualify you from being loved by God.

God can't run out of grace. Ever.

Why not confess your sins right now? Get them off your chest and tell God everything. He already knows—He's just waiting for you to ask. I promise He'll do it.

I have a strange calling on my life. I feel called to round up the devil's herd. God sent me to talk to the ones who don't think they are good enough for Him and those who have been running away from Him. He sent me to the ones who have lived a hard life—for whatever reason—and feel like it might be too late.

In the Bible you will find dozens of men and women who committed every kind of sin. Noah was an alcoholic. David was an adulterer and accessory to murder. Rahab (David's great-great-great-grandmother) was a prostitute. Zacchaeus was a corrupt tax collector. The apostle Paul (a.k.a. Saul of Tarsus) was a brutal persecutor of Christians. Peter betrayed Jesus . . . and the list goes on. But their sins didn't disqualify them.

Soon after I got out of prison, I was asked to share a message with a group of pastors. I was really nervous, and I went to God and said, *It's ten minutes until the curtain opens. Are they going to listen to this felon? Really? Maybe I should just cancel.*

God answered, *Listen, I know another felon convicted of something He never did. He received the death penalty.*

Yeah? I asked. *Who?*

That felon was My Son, Jesus.

Whoa! I never thought of it like that before!

And you know what? God said. *There were two convicted criminals hanging there beside Him. One mocked Jesus and said, "Aren't You supposed to be the Son of God? Why don't You save Yourself?" But the other one said, "Remember me when You come into Your Kingdom."*

"Remember me," I said out loud.

Jesus took that felon with Him. The first person into paradise after Jesus' death was a convicted felon. God is in the felony restoration business, and He certainly wants to restore you.

If you aren't sure what to say, start here: *Lord, remember me.*

That's a start. Praying *remember me* is a seed of faith. It means you believe—even if just a tiny little bit. So now, you can take it a little bit further.

Lord,

  I know I am a sinner and can do nothing to save myself. I cannot work my way to heaven; I can only get there through You. I believe You are the Son of God.

Even if I don't understand how it works yet, I believe You died on the cross to forgive my sins.

Remember me.

I want to be forgiven. I confess my sins. I repent, and I ask for Your forgiveness. By faith, I receive the gift of salvation. Help me learn to trust You. Come live in my heart and give me a new life.

In Jesus' name, amen.

Did you mean those words when you read them? If you did, then I want you to say them out loud. Confess with your mouth that Jesus is Lord. You believe what you hear yourself say. So say "Jesus is Lord" out loud right now.

Now say it again.

Say it until you believe it. Really believe it. "Jesus is Lord!"

Welcome to the pack! You now belong to my family—the family of God. God loves you, and He wants to see your life made new. He has a never-ending supply of second chances. Nine lives are nothing to Him!

I wish I could tell you that praying this prayer would fix everything for you by tomorrow, but that isn't true. The circumstances of your life may take some time to change. For sure, though, you will change. In the middle of your circumstances, God will change you. When you accept Jesus, you gain access to God's power and all the resources of heaven. You can ask Him for *anything*. You can call on Him for help in the middle of any kind of trouble. You can ask Him for miracles, just like I have done again and again, and God has never failed me yet.

I'm still changing. I drop the f-bomb a lot less these days. Francie says it is God sanding off my rough edges. But the real change is how I see God and love others. I can see God is changing me from the inside out. Whatever time I have left on this earth, I want to spend it loving God and loving people. I would rather have Jesus than fame. Fame is fleeting—it can vanish in a day. Salvation is forever.

If you just prayed that prayer for the first time—or maybe for the first time in a long time—I would love to hear from you. Will you please share this moment with me? You can email me at hello@dogthebountyhunter.com, and I will write back and send you some things that will encourage you and help you with your newly found or newly restored faith.

This chapter is called "Dog's Invitation," but it is really God's invitation. How will you answer?

I hope you'll say, "Remember me," so you can begin your new life too.

AFTERWORD

The LORD executes righteousness
and justice for all who are oppressed.

—Psalm 103:6

"DOG! HAVE YOU HEARD?"

It was Tonja Balden calling me. She was one of Andrew Luster's victims, and we keep in touch.

"Heard what? What's going on?" I asked. I could tell she was upset.

"I just finished giving my victim impact statement at Luster's parole hearing," she answered.

"They aren't granting him parole, are they?" I asked in disbelief. "They can't! That's impossible!"

"No. The California Department of Corrections and Rehabilitation Parole Board denied him, but it doesn't matter. It's worse than that," she said, then sighed.

"What could be worse than him getting out on parole?"

"He's just getting out. Released. They are releasing Andrew Luster on October 31, 2026," she said. I could hear the emotion in her voice.

"No. No way. That can't be right . . . How?" I think I was just as shocked as she was.

"I even spoke to Anthony Wold after the hearing. [Mr. Wold was the senior Ventura County district attorney who prosecuted Luster.] I wanted to know how it was possible that a release date had been set for him without any of his victims knowing about it."

"Oh, Tonja," I said, "I'm so sorry. I don't understand."

"It's bad enough that his sentence got reduced down to fifty years, and now this . . ." Her voice trailed off.

In 2013, Luster's attorney filed a petition—habeas corpus (or recourse in law for unlawful imprisonment)—and managed to get him a resentencing hearing because the trial judge from his original case failed to state his specific reasons for having imposed consecutive sentences. Even though his conviction stood, Luster's sentence was reduced by seventy-four years.

"When they reduced his sentence, I understood that it was supposed to be fifty years without the possibility of parole. I was furious but figured it still meant life in prison for him and that I never had to deal with him walking free during my lifetime either. The parole hearing already shook me. But now he'll be out? He will have served less than half of even that reduced sentence when they release him—he will skip one hundred years of his sentence! Dog, I can't believe this!"

I held my phone in my hand, wanting to answer her, but I didn't know what to say. I stood there stunned, trying to take in what Tonja was telling me. "Well, how is it possible that he could get out early if they denied his parole?" I asked.

"It's because of Proposition 57," she said.

"What? What do you mean? I thought Proposition 57 was meant to let *nonviolent* criminals earn credits for early parole. How does that help Luster?"

"That's what I thought too," Tonja answered. "Oh God—I voted *for* Proposition 57! I thought it was only to help guys who committed petty crimes and got stuck with unfair mandatory minimums get a fair shake. *Everything* I read about it made it seem like it was the decent thing to do. Humane and . . . well, a good thing!"

"I still don't understand." I shook my head. "Andrew Luster

didn't commit any petty crimes; he was convicted for rape—eighty-six counts of it. How does Prop 57 do anything for him?"

"It turns out that there is a loophole in the law. Yes, rape is a violent crime. It's still a violent crime. But rape with an unconscious person and some other things he was charged with are not specifically listed in the original California Penal Code. The loophole in Proposition 57 limits violent crimes to only the twenty-three specific crimes listed in the original code.[1] That means a lot of what Luster was convicted for has been reclassified as non-violent crimes."

"Oh my God!" I exclaimed. "I had no idea . . ."

"Dog, I will always and forever be grateful to you for catching him. I never dreamed in a million years we would be talking about him getting out," she said.

The case that put Dog the Bounty Hunter on the map always interests fans, and the fact that California voters have adopted Proposition 57, whose provisions are going to let this guy walk free, means I felt compelled to talk about Andrew Luster. I don't want the world to forget about him. Many of my new fans have never heard his name. This book is not about that famous hunt, but I wanted to share some of the story with those of you who are less familiar with the biggest bounty we never collected, even after capturing America's number one fugitive.

You can find the full account of this high-profile case with all the incredible details in my book *You Can Run but You Can't Hide.* What I present here is more of a highlight reel, along with my thoughts concerning Luster's early release.

Andrew Luster, heir to the Max Factor cosmetics fortune, was all over the news. Two years after his arrest, he was finally on trial, still walking around free on a one-million-dollar bond (reduced from the original ten million dollars). While the trial was still underway, before closing arguments and before a verdict or sentencing, Luster disappeared. The trial continued in absentia (in his absence), and Andrew Luster made the FBI's Top Ten Most Wanted list.

Luster was sentenced to 124 years in prison after being found guilty on eighty-six of eighty-seven charges, including rape, rape by the use of drugs, rape of an unconscious person, sexual battery, sodomy, poisoning, drug possession . . . . Luster had a pattern of giving girls GHB (gamma hydroxybutyrate), also known as "Liquid X," mixed with alcohol to make them compliant with his advances. Even more perverse, he gave them high enough doses to render them unconscious, then videotaped himself doing disgusting, criminal, perverted sexual acts to them so he could enjoy watching it later.

GHB, the "date rape drug," disappears completely from the bloodstream within twelve hours, so it is difficult to catch on a toxicology screen and prove. And it is such a powerful depressant and anesthetic that victims have zero memories of anything happening to them or being done to them while under its influence. Luster played the charming suitor while his victims were awake and treated them like his personal playthings when they were unconscious.

The girls we know about were assaulted by him hundreds of times without their consent (or knowledge). It wasn't until a woman got suspicious and recorded a call where Luster admitted giving her Liquid X that police got an arrest warrant and searched his house. The search uncovered the videotapes, the GHB, and other drugs. There were at least seventy-five women on those tapes, but only three could be identified and located. Those women did not learn they were victims until police brought them in and showed them the tapes. They had to witness themselves on-screen being violated while unconscious. Horrifying.

Once I learned about Luster and decided to join the hunt, I was soon doing news interviews everywhere. After an interview with Geraldo Rivera, I met Tonja Balden's husband. She was pregnant with twins during the trial, and the stress caused her to miscarry one of them. Her husband's torment jacked me up—I was ready to catch Luster no matter what it took. I was ready to do it for Tonja!

The next day, I appeared on *The Rita Cosby Show* and found myself face-to-face with Luster's defense attorney. I announced to the world that I was looking for Andrew Stuart Luster, and I intended to see him brought to justice. I honestly had no idea what I was getting myself into, but I vowed in front of everyone that I was going to catch him, so I was committed.

As always, I started the hunt by praying and asking God to point me in the right direction. We followed up by doing all the usual research to understand the guy—what he wanted, what he needed, who his friends were, and what his weaknesses were. The more information you have about him, the better your chances are of finding him. I came across a group of his friends who called themselves "the bachelor boys," and they all pointed me to search for Luster in Thailand. Luster had access to a lot more money than most of the guys I chase, so with those kinds of resources, I knew he would not likely stay inside the country, making him that much harder to track.

The victims' identities were secret, but we had already connected with Tonja, and Beth's resourcefulness led her to one more. These women wanted him found badly enough to share what they knew with us. I obtained a copy of the arrest warrant and mug shots from the Ventura County Court—a miracle because I had no authority to request them.

The more I learned, the more stunned I was that he had pled not guilty and continued to assert his innocence. I was dumbfounded that he had shown no remorse whatsoever. His own video cameras had caught him red-handed, yet he still held to his innocence. With each day, my resolve to track him down grew.

Rita Cosby called me back in for a follow-up interview. It was now June 9, 2003, and I felt no closer than I had during the first interview when I was so full of confidence. The search had now gone on for more than five months, and it took a toll on our family and our business. It kept Beth and me in separate locations, still trying to run our bail bond businesses and pay the bills. All the expenses for chasing Luster were coming out of my pocket. We didn't yet have a television show; we had only filmed episodes for some other shows at that point.

As a boxer, I always got beaten up in the first few rounds. *Ding-ding!* The bell ending round one sounded, and as I went to my corner, my coach would say, "You okay? I thought you came to box!"

I would go in for round two, and once again, I was a punching bag for my opponent until *Ding-ding!* ended the round. Back in my corner, my coach would get right in my face. "You okay, son?"

"Yeah, Coach, I'm good!" I'd nod and take a big drink of water.

"Aw, I'm glad to hear that . . ." Then he would smack my head and say, "Now, listen—you are playing around in there! Quit playing, get in there, and knock this guy out—you understand me?"

Sometimes it took three or even four rounds. I was never an early starter, but at some point, when the coach got in my face—boom! Something would come over me. I would rise, shake my head, lower my gaze, snort, and come out fighting like a man on fire. "Rip him in half!" my coach'd yell. And I would.

It was the same way on a hunt. I would go one, two, three, four days, and it was just like when I was boxing. I was in there; you weren't gonna knock me down, but the "thing" had not yet come over me. Beth used to look for it. She knew it when she saw it. She would say, "Do you feel it yet?"

"No," I answered.

The next day, she'd ask again, "Big Daddy, do you feel it yet?"

"Not yet."

Next day: "How about today? Do you feel it yet?"

Boom! There it was. It would come over me like liquid lightning, and when it did, nothing could get in my way. I now know it was the Spirit of God. Even then, I knew when it happened the hunt was all but over. "Yaaaaayyyy!" Beth would clap when she saw it. "You got him now!" And I would go get my man.

When I showed up for that second interview with Rita, I had not yet felt the "thing." As we came to the close of the segment and she asked me what I wanted to say to Andrew Luster—boom! There it was. The liquid lightning poured through me, and I looked straight into the camera and said, "Fe-fi-fo-fum. Look out, Luster, here I come!" I wanted him to know I was coming. And then I committed to catching him in ten days.

Beth thought I had lost my mind. Now I either caught him

in ten days, or our celebrity career as bounty hunters was over before it could begin. With the world watching and my reputation on the line, I prayed to God and asked for His help to track down Andrew Luster.

A tip came in. But this time, it was a solid lead. A man had met a guy calling himself Carrera (which in Spanish means "race" or "to run"). He was telling people he was a surfer from Hawaii. I think he chose Hawaii because he knew I was from Hawaii and that I was after him. He was twisted like that. But this tipster had photos of him—the photos looked like Luster!

We tracked him down to a villa north of Puerto Vallarta where he had partied with—you guessed it—GHB. More photos and more conversations with the villa owners convinced me we had found Luster. Beth persuaded Howard Schultz to finance tickets for Tim, Leland, Boris, and me to Mexico and send us a skeleton film crew to video Luster's takedown.

Schultz had no idea how close to bankruptcy we were, so we desperately needed him to finance this hunt in Mexico. The clock was ticking, and the media was keeping tabs on our progress— and our lack of progress. Once in Mexico, Howard kept in contact with retired agents in the FBI and also the CIA. A few days later, John Walsh showed up in Puerto Vallarta with *America's Most Wanted*. My leads were helping other hunters zero in, and some had more resources and backing than I did.

A few days later, Howard pulled out, no longer confident we would get our man. He left us with one cameraman, Jeff. I began to feel desperate when the people we stayed with changed their stories. I knew they had tipped Luster off. I prayed for God to send us a break in the case, which He did.

We found Luster and followed him to a taco stand, where we

took him down. He tried to run, but Leland went for his legs, Tim went for his neck, and I grabbed him around the waist. It was no contest—we had our man! I called Beth to tell her the good news. As we talked, we came up to a checkpoint. We gave our names, but Andrew Luster lied and said his name was David Carrera. He accused us of kidnapping him. Beth heard it all.

I protested that he was lying and showed them the notebook with the warrant for his arrest and mug shots, but they arrested us all—Leland, Tim, Boris, Jeff, and me—and we were tossed in a Mexican jail cell. The Federales saw us as criminals. They charged us with kidnapping—even *after* they confirmed that our story was true, and they called the FBI to come get Andrew Luster. The conditions in the jail were horrible, and I felt terrible that I had gotten the boys into this mess.

Whoever built the Huntsville Unit must have built this place. The smell was the same. It had the same walls, the same bars, the same keys—even the same paint. Memories flooded me, and I couldn't stand that the boys were locked up in here.

"Leland," I said, "all of you, listen. I am gonna take the rap. I will say it was all me. I am used to this; you guys can't be in here. I'm gonna make sure they let you go."

"No, you're not," Leland said.

"We're not gonna let you do that," Tim echoed.

"No way, man" was the consensus. I was stunned. Touched that they were behind me like that.

Inside the jail, we had no idea of the media attention on our case. We just knew we were dirty, tired, and being treated like the lowest of criminals. I had to draw on my faith, which seemed little more than a tiny grain of sand at this point. But as I gathered the boys in a circle, we each brought our single grain-of-sand faith together. There must have been enough faith between the five of us to make up that mustard seed because our lawyer showed up and informed us that the kidnapping charges had been reduced to deprivation of liberty. This was essentially a misdemeanor according to Mexican law. Such relief! We were liberated from jail—only to be thrown back in for violating immigration laws. It was torture.

Eventually, we were released on bail and permitted to stay in a Westin hotel while things got cleared up. That first shower felt so good; I will remember it as long as I live. Our spirits were lifted when we met so many friendly Americans at the hotel who welcomed us warmly and seemed to have been following the case.

Stacy Gilbert (ex-wife of Rick Allen, drummer for Def Leppard) introduced herself to us and offered her help. She was willing to drive us out of there, but there was no way we would put her in that position. She sat by me in the lobby and pulled up stories from the American media that demonstrated the world had not forgotten about us. It was very encouraging.

Our hotel bill climbed as the stay extended until it became absolutely necessary to adjust our living situation. We convinced the Mexican court to allow us to rent an apartment. We remained under house arrest and were not allowed to leave the city.

Luster got deported, but we were still detained.

There was a photo of me on the front page of a Mexican newspaper—Leland still has a copy of it. Next to my photo, the headline read (in Spanish, of course), "If You See This Man, Buy Him a Drink!" The story told how I brought my family with me to Mexico to chase down a low-life rapist and had been arrested for kidnapping and that we were still there being held under house arrest. The Mexican authorities didn't think much of us, but everywhere we went, the people of Mexico loved us.

One night, I dreamed of a helicopter descending into the prison compound. In my dream, President Bush had sent it for us. He stuck up for us. When I woke up, I asked God what the dream meant.

Months later, twenty-nine congressmen would send letters to then Secretary of State Condoleezza Rice asking her to deny extradition to Mexico for us. She was under enormous pressure because of drug cartel attacks on US facilities in Mexico. Later, the helicopter from my dreams would touch down and bring prisoners out of a Mexican jail, but I didn't know any of that when I awoke from my dream.

Go! I heard God say. *Go now! Run!*

God, I'm a bounty hunter; I don't run. Since when do You tell people to run?

Immediately, I remembered that an angel appeared to Joseph in a dream and told him to take Mary and baby Jesus and run to Egypt. If God could warn Joseph to get the heck out of Bethlehem, I guess He could tell me to get the hell out of Mexico!

So we decided to make a run for it. We didn't trust the Mexican authorities to give us a fair shake, and we didn't want to be stuck down there forever. We had to check in with the court every day, morning and evening, but not on the weekends. We convinced our lawyer to travel with us so that if we got caught, we could say we were just having a meeting with counsel. We waited until our 5:00 p.m. check with the court on Friday, then we fled.

All of us were deeply tanned, so if we kept our lighter-colored hair out of sight, we could blend in pretty easily with the locals.

We made it through a few checkpoints, and once outside of Puerto Vallarta, we stopped at a Burger King for cheeseburgers. As we were ordering, the news was on the television, flashing our pictures everywhere. We tried to act cool, but it was so obvious it was us that it is a wonder no one stopped us.

Our next stop was the airport. I just wanted out of there, but Leland had collected souvenirs of our stay. He had a pile of newspaper articles, our original airline tickets to Mexico, and even cigarillos from our stay inside the prison.

"You are gonna get us busted," I told him. But Leland had a plan!

He soaked his socks and underwear in the hotel bathroom sink and got them wet, then he put all the items on the bottom of his bag and the wet underwear on the top. When we got to the airport, we handed the guards our American passports and tickets, and miraculously, no one stopped us. Sure enough, the guard flagged Leland's bag.

I held my breath.

The guard unzipped the bag, but the moment he picked up that wet underwear, he threw it down like it was a snake! He made a disgusted face, snorted at Leland, and zipped the bag shut. We did it!

We flew to Tijuana, a little closer to the border, where our lawyer had arranged for a cab to pick us up curbside and get us across the border. We were all nervous as we pulled into the town and approached the crossing. Just then, an electric razor inside Leland's bag started vibrating.

"Leland!" I shouted. "You really are gonna get us all caught!"

Our driver had misplaced his pass, so he was busy rummaging under his seat, looking in the glove compartment, and not looking up. A policeman flagged us down, shouting "Alto! Alto!" while waving his machine gun, but the driver didn't see him!

I was sure he was setting us up and thought he was playing a ruse to get us captured and keep us from touching American soil. "Go! Gun it!" I shouted, and with my left foot, I pushed his foot on the gas pedal and punched it!

We sped through the crossing, and the moment we were through, we jumped out of the cab and ran as fast as we could to reach American soil.

The cab driver followed us and pulled up, smiling and waving papers in his hand. *"¡Mira, aquí tengo los papeles!"* (See, I have the papers here!) Our adrenaline was pumping as we escaped Mexico, and we hurried to climb back into the van and head to San Diego.

Not too far down the road, lights and sirens came up behind us. Fear gripped us all. *Are they going to send us back?* I wondered. "Out of the vehicle! Put your hands where I can see them!" an officer shouted. We got out slowly, and he shouted, "Freeze! Put that cigarette out; I can already charge you with attempted murder!"

"What?" I shook my head. "I don't understand!"

"Dog?" the officer said, holding his flashlight up and pointing at my face. Then he pointed it at my son. "Leland? . . . Oh my God! It's you! Welcome back to America!"

They gave us a police escort all the way to Los Angeles. God bless the USA!

Of course, getting back to the United States was just the beginning. It would be years before things were settled and behind us. Even in America, we were degraded and forced to wear ankle monitors like criminals while the charges from Mexico followed us around. We were in and out of court, racking up legal bills and always looking over our shoulders, wondering if we would be extradited to Mexico.

I never got paid the bounty I was owed for the capture of Andrew Luster. I never even got the reward promised by the FBI for information that led to his capture. Because we pursued him to Mexico—where the laws are different, and we didn't have legal authority as bounty hunters—there were enough loopholes for the authorities to wriggle free. They could not deny we had been the ones who tracked down, found, and captured Andrew Luster. They used technicalities to keep us from collecting what was promised.

For better or for worse, Andrew Luster was the case that launched me into the success of the *Dog the Bounty Hunter* television series. I was forged in the flame. My name became a household word, and the image of my face was everywhere. I cannot measure how many doors of opportunity have been opened for me because the capture of Andrew Luster provided me with a key.

God works all things for my good.[2]

It is good that both justice and mercy are in the hands of God.

It is hard for me to think about mercy regarding Andrew Luster. I think about his victims. I think about how he threw his money around, defied the law, and had no regard for the women he hurt. To my knowledge, he has still never admitted his guilt or demonstrated any remorse for his actions.

I wonder if when California voters chose to pass Proposition 57 in 2016, they had any idea of the consequences it would bring. The marketing that sold it to the people was good enough to convince Tonja Balden that it was a good law. She had no idea it would free her attacker. Andrew Luster will be in his early sixties when he is released—the sole heir to that huge fortune, his to enjoy.

At the time of this writing, Luster has been in prison for roughly twenty years, and that hardly seems enough time. My heart embraces his victims. I believe in second chances for everyone. I have had my share, so I genuinely hope Luster's time in prison has changed him. I hope he has been brought face-to-face with his Maker and understands that he will answer for his actions either in this life or in the life that comes after.

I will keep one eye on Andrew Luster for as long as I draw breath. God has forgiven me so much that I hesitate to stand in judgment of who and what He forgives for others.

I leave you to think about this verse:

> *When justice is served,*
> *the lovers of God celebrate and rejoice,*
> *but the wicked begin to panic.*[3]

God is a God of justice, and eternity is a long, long time. God will settle the books. He is the only One who knows the whole story. The righteous will reap their rewards, and the wicked will reap their whirlwind. When all is said and done, I have to trust in God's justice.

ACKNOWLEDGMENTS

DID THERE NEED TO BE A THIRD BOOK ABOUT MY LIFE? SOME of you might think not. However, the first two were bestsellers and yet, they didn't share enough about the most important element of my life: my walk with God. This book is the most important one I've published yet.

I've done my best to recall origin stories as accurately as possible, but I know my memory is likely not infallible. Any errors are mine and mine alone.

I want to thank first of all my Lord and Savior Jesus Christ for His provision and saving grace. If He can use someone like me, He can use anyone! I'm especially grateful to Francie for her encouragement. I love you so much, Francie, and am so thankful He brought us together.

I want to acknowledge my children, whom I love. I pray for you every day and each of you is a gift to me from the Lord.

Thank you as well to my team who makes it all happen as well as the incomparable publishing staff at Nelson Books—thank you for believing in me. Most of all, I want to thank the fans who inspire me to keep going. I love you all.

NOTES

INTRODUCTION

1. Proverbs 18:21.
2. Phil Lander et al., *Dog and Beth: Fight of Their Lives*, performance by Duane Chapman and Beth Chapman, A&E, November 27, 2017.
3. Lander et al., *Dog and Beth*.
4. Luke 8:52 NIV.
5. 2 Kings 20:17–18 NIV.
6. 2 Kings 20:19 NIV.
7. Mark 16:15 NIV.

CHAPTER ONE: PUPPY PAINS

1. 1 Corinthians 14:31.
2. John 14:14 KJV.
3. "Celebrate Bible Translation Day!," Wycliffe Bible Translators, September 1, 2020, https://www.wycliffe.org/blog/posts /celebrate-bible-translation-day.
4. Mark 5:15, Luke 8:35, paraphrased.
5. 1 Corinthians 12:7–11, especially verse 8 that talks about "the word of knowledge."

6. Daniel 3:25.

7. 1 Corinthians 12:4–11.

8. John 10:10.

9. Psalm 56:8.

CHAPTER TWO: BECOMING DOG

1. Luke 15:11–32.

2. 1 Samuel 13:14; Acts 13:22.

CHAPTER THREE: CAGED DOG

1. Matthew 27:5 KJV.

2. John 21:17 KJV.

CHAPTER FOUR: RELEASED DOG

1. Malachi 3:8 KJV.

2. Romans 12:19 KJV.

CHAPTER FIVE: HUNTING DOG

1. Matthew 7:16 KJV.

2. Romans 11:29.

3. See, for example, Jeremiah 1:5–7, where God appointed Jeremiah as a prophet before he was born.

4. Romans 11:29 NLT and KJV, respectively.

5. For the full story, read Exodus 1:15–21 NIV.

CHAPTER SIX: DADDY DOG

1. Proverbs 22:6 KJV.

CHAPTER SEVEN: TOP DOG

1. Isaiah 55:11.

2. Isaiah 55:11.

3. Proverbs 13:20 MSG.

4. Proverbs 18:21 KJV.

5. Proverbs 27:17.

6. Matthew 10:33 KJV.

7. "Meet the Chapmans," *Dog the Bounty Hunter,* season 1, episode 1, A&E, aired August 30, 2004.

8. 1 Peter 5:6–8.

CHAPTER EIGHT: CAN'T KEEP A GOOD DOG DOWN

1. 2 Corinthians 10:5 NIV, NLT, and NKJV, respectively.

2. For the transcript of my interview with Larry King, see "'Dog's' Reputation: How Badly Hurt?," *Larry King Live*, aired November 7, 2007, https://transcripts.cnn.com/show/lkl/date /2007-11-07/segment/01.

3. "'Dog's' Reputation."

4. Song of Solomon 8:6–7 KJV, emphasis added.

5. 1 Corinthians 15:55 MEV.

CHAPTER NINE: DOG'S NEW DAY

1. See "Duane 'Dog the Bounty Hunter' Chapman Is Engaged," FOX 5 San Diego, May 4, 2020, https://fox5sandiego.com /entertainment/duane-dog-the-bounty-hunter-chapman-is -engaged/.

2. Luke 18:27 NIV.

3. Genesis 2:18.

CHAPTER TEN: DIGGING UP BONES

1. This is not her real name. Her name has been changed to respect her privacy.

2. Matthew 20:16.

3. John 16:20.

4. Deuteronomy 28:2.

CHAPTER ELEVEN: DOG'S NEXT HUNT

1. See Genesis 4:1–15 for the whole story.

2. "'Bones' Found at North Port Reserve Belong to Brian Laundrie: FBI," FOX 13 Tampa Bay, October 22, 2021, https://www.fox13news.com/news/bones-found-at-north-port-reserve-belong-to-brian-laundrie-family-lawyer-confirms.

3. Aya Elamroussi, et al., "Dental Records Show Remains Found at Carlton Reserve Are Those of Brian Laundrie, FBI Says," CNN, October 21, 2021, https://www.cnn.com/2021/10/21/us/brian-laundrie-update-gabby-petito-thursday/index.html.

4. Elamroussi et al., "Dental Records Show."

5. Walt Buteau, "Retired FBI Agent Wonders About Brian Laundrie's 'Bothersome' Final Decision," NBC 8 Tampa Bay, February 25, 2022, https://www.wfla.com/8-on-your-side/retired-fbi-agent-wonders-about-brian-laundries-bothersome-final-decision/.

6. Exodus 32:1–14.

7. "Miss Teacher Bangs a Boy," *South Park*: Season 10, Episode 10, 2006.

8. Lamentations 3:22–23.

CHAPTER TWELVE: DOG'S INVITATION

1. Psalm 51:10–12 KJV.

2. Micah 7:19.

3. Psalm 103.

AFTERWORD

1. "Penal Code-PEN, Part 1 of Crimes and Punishments
   [25-680.4], Title 16. General Provisions [654-678]. 667.5,"
   California Legislative Information, accessed March 29, 2023,
   https://leginfo.legislature.ca.gov/faces/codes_displaySection
   .xhtml?lawCode=PEN&sectionNum=667.5.

2. Romans 8:28.

3. Proverbs 21:15 TPT.

ABOUT THE
AUTHOR

DUANE LEE CHAPMAN, ALSO KNOWN AS DOG THE BOUNTY Hunter, is an American television personality known for popular TV programs that follow his life and adventures as a bounty hunter. Dog is deeply involved in crime fighting and advocating for tougher legislation to curb crime. He is launching several media ventures, including a new TV show and podcast, and he is a *New York Times* bestselling author of two previous books. Dog operates Light Up the Darkness ministry with his wife, Francie, whom he married in 2021. They reside in Florida.